life, re purposed

Stories of Grace, Hope, and Restored Faith

life, repurposed

Stories of Grace, Hope, and Restored Faith

Foreword by *Jane Rubietta*

Compiled and Edited by Michelle Rayburn

FAITH CREATIVITY LIFE BOOKS

Friend —
May you be
reminded you are
a CHERISHED TREASURE
in Christ!
Annette Warsaw
Ps. 139 p. 33 !! ☺

Contents

Foreword

Jane Rubietta

Upcycling and repurposing frighten me. I am neither crafty nor particularly coordinated. I numb out at DIY shows, bewildered by their billions of viewers. Painting dressers and slathering decoupage renders me glassy-eyed. I rarely see furniture and think, "I could repurpose this as . . ." although I do keep broken things in hope that someone will be able to work magic. I hold in awe those skilled visionaries.

When I was growing up, all gangly and awkward, the myth of the perfect home and family held such allure in my high-decibel and chaotic life. My best friend and her family boated and skied and redecorated rooms in snappy trendy colors. She sewed and baked, tutored by her trim and energetic mother. I got in on the action as often as possible, and we held slumber parties in our flannel-lined sleeping bags with calmness all around and also, thank you very much, hot cookies.

At age nine, I didn't know what could be behind the scenes. I only knew my own behind-closed-doors truth. Likely, life in that family wasn't nearly as perfect as it felt. That myth, that the perfect home and life are achievable, eventually merged with the images of the godly Christian home lauded from the pulpits and study groups of people I loved and admired. By then, as a young adult following after God, I nodded in vehemence. That would be me. That would be my future husband. Together, we'd break the chains of the past and create that little oasis of perfection.

Not long into adulthood, my perfect little hopes crashed into the dead-end alley of reality. Life wasn't perfect. I wasn't the perfect *anyone*— not woman, wife, mother, friend, or leader. Even bigger, I didn't know how to reconcile my own difficult past and current problems, with the Jesus who was supposed to help a sister out. I just wanted the magic to take over.

This Christianity stuff just didn't work. I nearly walked away from Jesus. Honestly, I tried, but he wasn't having it and kept following me. When shame tried to strangle me (after all, I'm a pastor's wife, mother, woman in ministry, and leader), Jesus awakened me to the realization that healing is possible with his help, and good can emerge from bad.

But Jesus refused to let me stop there. Transformation, it turns out, is not for my sake only. Jesus changes us for the good of others.

That's great, right? But the problem with personal problems is they are so very personal, and thus isolating. We feel alone, ashamed, and too often frightened. From there, it's not a big leap to land on failure as a woman.

In *Life, Repurposed*, you will be surrounded by women like you. You'll meet such courageous people, whose stories do not end with their travail. Whether headlines come home, or heartache is personal, through their words, one truth rises. No, two:

Troubles are inevitable.

Transformation is possible.

There is a pathway forward through the pain, through the regret. These women stay in the struggle and opt for transformation. Their willingness to wrest good from hardship requires courage and strength and determination, and the certainty that God's power is made perfect in weakness. Here, there is no shame, no myth, no magic. Rather, thirty-four sets of hands to hold as you stare down your regrets and discover resilience you didn't know you possessed. You're in good company.

No personal strength required. Bring your weakness, and let God be strong. Talk about perfect.

Regardless of your particular struggle, you'll find hope here. It's the ultimate repurposing: our hardships result in hope for others.

And, even more good news: no crafts or coordination required. (Though I do have a chair I wanted to ask you about.)

Jane Rubietta

Jane Rubietta writes about hard stuff with hope and a whole lot of honesty. Through her many books and speaking, she helps people find value in seemingly senseless difficulties, moving through transition into transformation. Thankfully, she's hilarious; otherwise this wouldn't be any fun. Books include her debut novel *The Forgotten Life of Evelyn Lewis* (Surprise! It's about repurposing the past!) and *Brilliance: Finding Light in Dark Places.* More at JaneRubietta.com

Introduction

Michelle Rayburn

When the idea of a repurposed life first sparked something in me, I was a blogger who decorated my home on the cheap with thrift-sale finds. I'd post photos and tutorials to show others how they could turn junk into treasure too. Behind the laptop, I was a stay-at-home mom with two active boys who also loved the thrill of rummaging through other people's stuff on makeshift tables set up in back alleys and garages for city-wide sales. They hunted for video games and books while I browsed the household cast-offs and rusty garden tools.

As I transformed the fifty-cent and five-dollar bargains into candle holders and luminaries, wall art, and chalky finished accent pieces, I learned to appreciate the way discarded items gained new purpose through a little imagination and a few strokes of paint. It didn't take long to connect that passion with a life application—because everything's writing material if you ask me.

Hardships and disappointments come our way, pain caused by careless words or abusive intent cuts into our self-image, and tragedy too harsh to speak of pierces our courage and threatens to steal our confidence. But from the remains, we rise from heartbreak and press on, infused with the power of God, who repurposes tragedy into victory.

With a repurposed life, we release pride and selfishness, choosing compassion and humility instead. Emancipated from anger and resentment, we can rejoice over a renewed mind and resilient passion for helping others. Like my well-loved, repurposed treasures, our imperfections and scars become stories that tell of triumph over the trashy stuff of life. Where there was once shame, hope shines through. Where there was bitterness, love and forgiveness have taken over. Where there was emptiness, there is Jesus.

When I wrote my first book, *The Repurposed and Upcycled Life*, I told my own trash-to-treasure story, how God showed up amid my stinky attitude and frustrating circumstances and gave me new perspective—and how he continues to work on shaping me into a woman who reflects the character of Jesus. I'm a work in progress! Now it's time to share the incredible stories of other women who have experienced the beautiful transformation of a repurposed life.

In 2018, I launched the *Life, Repurposed* podcast, where I often interview guests who tell of what God has done in their lives. I soon realized there were so many more stories to tell—more renovated lives to celebrate. And so, the idea for *Life, Repurposed: Stories of Grace, Hope, and Restored Faith* was born.

We want our lives to point others to Jesus in such a way that the Master Designer and Repurposer gets all the glory. Our before and after should cause others who hear our stories to say, "Only God could bring about something that amazing." We bring the junk, and he works the renovation with his power and his abundant grace.

I've always been inspired by God's promise to Israel during tragic oppression:

. . . he will give a crown of beauty for ashes,
a joyous blessing instead of mourning,
festive praise instead of despair

Isaiah 61:3

As you read each story, listen for the hope, the joyous blessing that replaces broken hearts. Lean in and look for yourself in the pages. This kind of repurposed life—one marked by freedom from the past—is for you too. I've celebrated as I read each author's testimony. Praised God for his wonderful love and grace. Cried tears of joy for every victory of which they tell.

And now I pray earnestly for you, dear reader—that your heart will be stirred as you read. I hope you will pause to **renew and restore** at the end of each chapter, either on your own or with a group of friends. Let it change you and renew your mind. Bring on the repurposing!

May the love and grace of Jesus be with you and give you peace.

Michelle Rayburn, Editor

Anyone who belongs to Christ has become a new person.
The old life is gone; a new life has begun.

2 Corinthians 5:17

Michelle Rayburn appreciates how life's difficulties can turn out to be opportunities to learn and grow. She's the author of hundreds of articles and several Christian living books, including *Classic Marriage: Staying in Love When Your Odometer Climbs,* and *The Repurposed and Upcycled Life: When God Turns Trash to Treasure.* Michelle hosts a weekly podcast called *Life, Repurposed* to encourage women to find hope in life's trashy stuff. She enjoys dark chocolate, iced coffee, and a breezy afternoon in the hammock with a good book—preferably all three together. www.michellerayburn.com

The Treasured Hoosier Cabinet

Christina Ryan Claypool

Even as a little girl, I adored old-fashioned furniture. This was a good thing because my childhood home was filled with recycled items collected by my late mother. Once with her half-dozen children loaded in her old car, she spied a treasure amid the curbside trash at a residence close to our home. Mom gasped with pleasure, but I was sure the old bookshelf had seen better days. Not to be denied, my mother marched up to the front door and rang the bell. "Can I please have your bookcase?" she asked the elderly female owner.

The dark wood was heavily marred with scratches, and it didn't look like much of a prize.

Today, we would probably paint it to cover the imperfections. But in my mother's era, Old English furniture polish was the standard cure for distressed wood, so Mom doused the entire bookcase in the dark liquid. Almost magically, the polish seemed to breathe new life into it.

When the bookshelf dried, my mother covered the deep gouges on the top with a lace doily and then filled the shelves with books and glassware. Even though I had seen her do it countless times, once more, this resourceful woman created something magnificent out of someone else's junk.

This happened in an era when terms such as repurpose, restore, or reinvent didn't exist. There was no category of household items or furniture known as shabby chic or vintage, no stores filled with repurposed products. If something was old and used, it was simply that, "used." It was to be looked down upon, rejected, or devalued. Despite its age, if it was in less than perfect condition, an object became far less valuable. It was no longer considered a costly antique, but often it turned into worthless trash.

Learning by Example

My mother's lesson about reclaiming the beauty of a castoff item stayed with me. Her philosophy greatly contributed to my decision to open a thrift/antique store when I found myself going through a painful divorce decades later. Truthfully, I also felt like a jilted throwaway after being rejected by the spouse who had once promised to love and cherish me.

At the time, I was in my early thirties, and my little boy was only seven. As a single mom, I wanted Zachary to have a sense of security. My former jobs as a media reporter and later in corporate sales required long hours and would result in being away from him too much. That's why, after a lot of prayer about the future, my childhood dream of opening a retail secondhand shop seemed to miraculously resurrect. It was in desperation, not self-confidence, that I stepped out in faith to follow God's direction.

To fulfill this vision, I rented the bottom floor of an older home zoned commercial, using the front for the store. Zach and I made an apartment in a couple of rooms in the back. The only problem was, I didn't have any furniture other than my son's twin bed, his dresser, and a small kitchen table. I was starting over from scratch, leaving most of the furnishings in the home I had shared with my ex-husband.

In order to find merchandise for my store, I attended auctions, estate and garage sales, and was also blessed with donations from generous family and friends. The shop filled up almost supernaturally, despite my extremely limited budget. Still, there wasn't anything left over to afford much for our apartment.

An older woman from my church encouraged me as best she could. Shirley was in her sixties, and she took my little boy and me under her proverbial maternal wing. One day, she stopped to check on us, and I excitedly showed her the shop and apartment.

"Where's the furniture?" Shirley asked, looking around our conspicuously empty living quarters. There were tears of concern in her eyes.

"Don't worry," I said. "It's all here by faith. I can already see it." I tried my best to reassure her and myself, trusting—as the Bible encourages us to do—that God would provide. "Faith shows the reality of what we hope for, it is the evidence of things we cannot see" (Hebrews 11:1).

Answered Prayer

My faith was definitely childlike because I had finally turned my hot mess of a life over to my heavenly Father. A couple of years earlier, I had accepted Jesus as my Savior while battling depression on a psychiatric ward, but I didn't really make him Lord of my life.

Stubbornly, I kept controlling my circumstances and making poor choices, until my heart was shattered by my broken relationship. That's when I surrendered control and asked for God's help with every decision, desire, and need. My desperate prayers for my marriage to be healed weren't answered how I had hoped. Instead, God gave me the gift of opening the store.

Regarding my prayer for furniture, before long, there was a vintage couch and chair, a wicker desk, a comfortable bed and dresser for me, and even a TV. But one piece of furniture I dreamed of having didn't materialize. It was an antique two-piece cabinet I admired made by different manufacturers such as Hoosier and Sellers. I would see these cabinets in antique shops, at auctions and sales, and even flea markets, but I could never afford one.

That is, until the day I happened to stop at *Price's Used Furniture Store*. The retail outlet was more of a bargain basement for modern used furniture and appliances, so the stately cabinet from another era looked glaringly out of place.

"How much is the Hoosier cabinet?" I asked, sure it would be more than I could afford. I was shocked when Mr. Price, who was about my father's age, quoted a price of half the going rate everywhere else.

"It belongs to a young relative. She's getting divorced and needs to sell it," he said. Mr. Price explained the low price, citing the cabinet's multiple imperfections. Decades earlier, a rat, most likely, had chewed two small passageways into the cabinet door, and the porcelain work surface was missing. There was some cracked oak and a replaced glass piece that didn't match either.

The letters H-O-O-S-I-E-R stamped around the metal latch on the cabinet top were mostly visible though, verifying its authenticity. The bread drawer and flour bin were also intact with the date "Pat. Feb. 8, 1910" stamped in the metal door's opening.

February 8 was the day we celebrated my grandmother's birthday. Despite being in her early eighties, Grandma volunteered in my store as a clerk, waiting on customers, ironing inventory for endless hours, and babysitting Zach whenever she was needed. The store and our lives were so much better because of Gram's support. This made the date significant.

As for the cabinet's many flaws, my mother's philosophy of reclaiming lost beauty flooded over me. An antique dealer would assert that these imperfections devalued it immensely, but they only made me admire it more. It reflected my own complicated testimony of the immeasurable value of a repurposed life. I had been abandoned and rejected, broken beyond repair, but God's grace put me back together, and his redemptive glory shone through my formerly cracked places.

New Beginnings Abound

With my shop being established by then, purchasing the cabinet from another single mom in financial need, like I had once been, appeared to be divine intervention. The Hoosier fit perfectly into the spot waiting for it in my apartment. Besides being beautiful, the two-piece cupboard was incredibly useful since it was originally created to be a functional storage unit.

For several years, the oak piece sat regally in its place—until the day the former owner showed up in my store.

The middle-aged stranger explained her relation to Mr. Price, how the cabinet had once been hers, and she asked if I still had it.

"Yes, it's back in my apartment," I said, my heart sinking, assuming she might want it back.

"Could I please see it?" the brunette woman inquired. I couldn't refuse because I could tell from her eager tone, the cupboard meant as much to her as it did to me.

I walked her down the hallway and opened the apartment door. She stood speechless, lovingly gazing at her former possession.

"Do you want to buy it back?" I struggled to get the words out, understanding if she did, our benevolent Father would expect me to do the right thing.

"No . . . I just wanted to know it has a good home." She shared how there were complicated memories connected to the cabinet. Having experienced the tragedy of divorce myself, I understood how good memories can be tainted by bad ones, even when it comes to furniture. That's one reason I left everything a few years before to start over with a new beginning.

Now, many years have passed with the cabinet being part of countless additional memories. Memories of my son growing up, of holidays and birthdays, of me becoming a Christian author, of marrying again and carefully moving the two-piece cupboard four times for my husband's career.

After all, our merciful Maker is all about new beginnings. Through the changing seasons, I have discovered that due to our Creator's divine design for our lives, we can wait with expectancy in the midst of despairing circumstances. But I first learned about this promise as a young single mother fighting fear over what unexpected trouble tomorrow might hold.

As a reminder to keep the faith during turbulent times, I can cling to this verse about trusting in God's good intentions, "Do not be afraid or discouraged, for the LORD will personally go ahead of you. He will be with you; he will neither fail you nor abandon you" (Deuteronomy 31:8).

God has proven his steadfast faithfulness over and over.

I can't help but occasionally wonder who will own the cupboard next. Until then, I will cherish the gift of my treasured Hoosier cabinet for as long as it's mine. Hopefully, making lots more happy memories along the way.

Renew and Restore

- Remember back to a time when you prayed fervently for a specific answer from God. If the answer didn't come the way you expected, where could you still see God's provision?
- Imagine you have a loved one going through a painful divorce or another relationship issue. What could you do to support them?
- Is there a furniture item you have always wished you owned? How could you make that wish a reality without going into debt?

Christina Ryan Claypool is an award-winning journalist and Christian speaker who has been featured on *Joyce Meyer Ministries* TV show and CBN's *700 Club*. She is a four-time Chicken Soup for the Soul book contributor and has also authored several Christian recovery books. Her latest inspirational, *Secrets of the Pastor's Wife: A Novel*, is available at all major online outlets or through her website at www.christinaryanclaypool.com.

Delayed But Not Denied

Becky Hofstad

I *was supposed to be in* Kenya. The trip had been cancelled due to political unrest and violence there, but I took it personally. I believed God was shaking a deterring finger at me as I approached the trailhead for the path I thought I was supposed to take. I'd initiated looking for grant opportunities to aid a non-profit organization working to alleviate drought in Kenya. They provided saplings from their nursery to schools and churches that would plant and care for the trees. I interpreted the trip cancellation as a dead end.

I stood wilted, at a loss for what I was supposed to be doing with my single life. At thirty-eight, I'd shelved my hopes for meeting the love of my life. A *Newsweek* story published when I was in high school predicted white, college-educated women that were still single at forty would in all likelihood remain unmarried. It had haunted me ever since. As a professional woman, I spent too much time at work—and it certainly didn't feel like a calling—but what was God's purpose for me?

When the plug got pulled on Kenya, I immediately made an alternate plan to visit Southern California. I needed sunshine and an escape from

February in Minnesota, which was still firmly in the grip of winter. On the first evening, I walked down the sidewalk along Pacific Coast Highway and took in the energy of the waves crashing onto the shore. Long before I reached the heavy front door of BJ's, the aroma of fresh pizza was in the air. I knew spending time with friends I'd bonded with while earning a PhD in chemistry at UC Irvine would bring healing and perspective.

Gene and Daizy, already seated in a booth, were my first and only successful set-up attempt.

We chatted about my plans for the visit and exchanged updates on mutual friends before a deep-dish pizza loaded with pepperoni appeared in the center of our table. They prayed that our time would be a blessing. I felt comforted.

"So, Becky, do you think you're ever going to get married?" Gene asked, fumbling with a piece of pizza so that eye contact could be intermittent.

"You don't have to answer that," Daizy said as she shot Gene a scolding glance perfected by ten years of marriage.

"I'd like to be married. I really want someone to share my life with, but I can't seem to find him." I wiped my mouth, not sure whether some sauce had strayed.

"Where have you looked?" Gene prompted. The truth was that after years of praying, I'd mostly given up.

"What about doing more online dating?" Daizy suggested. Though my parents taught me with enough hard work I could reach any goal, my own efforts had gotten me nowhere in finding a life partner.

"I feel as if at my age all the good ones have been taken." I knew my expectations for a mate were high—some would say I was picky—but I wasn't willing to settle for less. In my mind, that would be a considerably worse fate.

Could It Be?

Two months later, I nearly missed my first date with Mike.

Driving to the restaurant, I asked myself why I'd agreed to another set-up, but a good friend from college had gone to the trouble of making the connection. She'd chatted with a pastor at her church in the copy room. When he mentioned that his single son had just returned from a mission trip and was now training for a triathlon, her ears perked up. The son and I exchanged a few emails. He suggested we meet for dinner.

After I'd waited for ten minutes at the entrance of an urban mall in Uptown Minneapolis, a nearly billboard-sized sign for the barbeque restaurant hanging high above, it dawned on me that the sign was not directly outside the restaurant itself. I hustled through the mall, panicked, half-wondering if my tardiness would be fate's rescue.

There he was, sitting on a bench in front of the barbeque restaurant entrance exactly as planned. As I approached, he put down the paper he'd been reading and stood up. His warm eyes spoke a hello, and I knew in an instant that I was glad he'd waited.

"You must be Becky," he said. I explained my mistake, tripping over my words only once, and apologized for being late. He smiled, unruffled, and suggested we check out the Thai restaurant around the corner.

As we talked over dinner, I was placing checkmarks in my mental list of "must haves" at a rapid rate. I noted questions to follow up on later. I tingled inside, excitement pulsing through my body. He cared about the environment. He was active in his church. We were both "savers," not "spenders." He wasn't all talk about living a healthy, active life. Where did he come from?

Nearly three hours passed without any pauses in our conversation, except to chew and exchange tastes of each other's dishes. Near the end of the evening, the topic of online dating came up.

"By my calculation, I've had about twenty-four first dates," he admitted.

"And none of those led to a second?"

"No." Mike cleared his throat before saying, "I remember one girl in particular. As we introduced ourselves, I could see by the look on her face it was over. I wished I'd said, 'Should we just call it a night right now?'"

I found his transparency refreshing.

A New Trail

Fifteen months later, Mike and I sat on a blanket in front of the famous Spoonbridge and Cherry sculpture, the side pocket of his shorts concealing a ring box-shaped bulge. "As we finished dinner at that Thai restaurant on our first date," he began, "I remember thinking to myself, 'Should I just ask this girl to marry me right now and skip all the goofing around?'" He looked deep into my eyes. "But our goofing around has been some of the best goofing around of my life. So I'm asking you now, would you become my wife and goof around with me for the rest of our lives?"

A cool breeze signaled evening was approaching as I agreed to spend the rest of my life with a man that was God's answer to many prayers.

Another Change in Plans

Before I left for the airport, four inches of snow overnight required that I clear the driveway. I scraped a metal shovel over the asphalt surface and thought about the last time I had been in Orange County. I'd gone to escape for a few days, unsure where my life was headed. Now a half-decade later, this time I would join my husband, my partner in the life purposes God had shown us.

My arrival signaled the end of Mike's week of collaborating with California co-workers. We were both ready to get outside. Saturday morning, blossoms of Birds of Paradise growing on an arbor welcomed us to the trailhead. We felt dwarfed by the expanse of mountains surrounding us as we settled into a hiking stride.

"I can't quite believe it's been five years since we had our first date." Mike said as he brought up one of the reasons for our trip. Celebrating our first date in some ways felt almost more significant than our wedding anniversary. It was the night we walked into our Narnia together, a world neither of us knew existed.

"Sometimes I have a hard time remembering what life was like before we met," I said. After we married, transforming Mike's bachelor pad into a home for the two of us was the first project we tackled together. For five months, we met at his house after work, stained woodwork or painted a room, then drove twenty minutes to my condo to sleep before doing it all over again the next day. We were busy but found decisions such as which medicine cabinet to put in the bathroom or whether we really needed a granite countertop in the kitchen were not contentious but came easily.

After we completed the renovations, we moved back in and got serious about starting a family. This second project didn't go as smoothly. We encountered one of the realities of marrying later in life: infertility.

As we rounded a switchback on our hike, Mike and I were both mindful of the next big transition in our life together. We were on the verge of stepping into parenthood. Three years spent on the path to adopting a child felt long and had required us to surrender control to God. I knew the wait would be worth it and was looking forward to becoming a mother soon.

"So, when do you think I should quit working?" I asked Mike.

We'd decided that bonding with our new daughter was a high priority. Some questioned how I could leave my career as a chemist behind. I knew the implication was, "after going to school for all those years."

It was true that God's purposes for my life were not what anyone had expected—especially me. I'd learned, over time and with a lot of prayer, to leave space for God to speak into what he wanted for my life instead of wandering off on my own.

Mike and I decided that I should quit working after we received the approval we needed from U.S. Citizenship and Immigration Services, which would allow us to bring Naomi to the U.S. While we waited for the last steps to be completed in Africa, I would have some time to paint the exterior trim of our house, get Naomi's room ready, and nest.

The California sun warmed me on the outside as anticipation for the next page turn of our story settled into my soul. Mike and I would travel to Africa soon to welcome five-year-old Naomi and become a family.

Our final evening in Orange County brought me full circle back to BJ's for a pizza dinner with Gene and Daizy. They hadn't aged a day since Mike and I saw them at our wedding.

"Do you guys remember what we talked about here on that night five years ago?" I asked.

"I think we talked about whether you were ever going to get married," Gene smirked before the rest of us laughed. I was satisfied to know that some of the questions I'd had back then about what direction my life was going to take had found some answers.

As we called it an evening, it occurred to me that what I had thought was Africa denied turned out to only be Africa delayed.

Renew and Restore

- "We can make our plans, but the LORD determines our steps" (Proverbs 16:9). How have you seen this verse play out in your life?
- How have you reacted when circumstances failed to line up with your expectations or goals?
- Where have you discovered hope and encouragement when plans are on hold?
- How can you be intentional about putting aside unhelpful messages encountered in society and the media related to your circumstances?
- In what current situation do you think you could use an outlook that gives God space to reveal his purposes?

Becky Hofstad lives with her husband, Mike, and two adopted daughters, Naomi and Tutu, in a suburb of Minneapolis. Becky loves to write about the ways God has worked in her life. One of these stories is published in *Short and Sweet: Angels in Disguise?* Her writing has been recognized with awards from the Minnesota Christian Writers Guild and Faith Radio. She is currently revising a memoir and can be reached at rebecca.hofstad@gmail.com.

From Gang Life
to Glorious Life

Maureen Hager

My mother secretly moved her belongings to an apartment while my sister, brother, and I were at school. Dad broke the news to us—she was never coming back. As a teenager, I developed a defiant attitude in my heart as I struggled to resist the feelings of abandonment and anger toward Mom leaving us.

A lack of emotional security at home caused me to search for love and acceptance outside of my family. This misguided quest lured me into a world of drugs and life in a motorcycle gang. As part of this outlaw family, I envisioned myself pledging my loyalty to the club and adopting their set of values. It was an illusion of freedom that required adopting a lifestyle of rebellion toward the mainstream culture.

Misguided Belonging

Gang life offered me the promise of excitement, endless drugs, and a sense of belonging. I became a part of this biker family, embracing the camaraderie of my new brothers and sisters. I was Viggo's "old lady," which meant I was his property. He gave the orders, and I obeyed.

I soon developed a false sense of security. It wasn't until I'd witnessed many injustices against others that I realized I was slipping into a dark world without hope. I had no idea how I would escape from the control the gang imposed on my life.

My answer came most unexpectedly. In the early morning hours, a rival gang armed with M16 rifles stood outside the clubhouse where we lived. I was standing in the doorway facing the front windows and silhouetted by light when the shooting started.

I was an easy target when the first bullets were fired.

As I reached for the light switch, I felt a fiery sensation in my left forearm that had covered my heart. I have no explanation as to why I used my left arm to turn on the light since the light switch was to my right. The Lord was my shield that night. He protected me from the rival gang that came to kill and destroy.

The impact of the bullets threw me face down. Before I hit the floor, another bullet lodged in my right thigh. My left arm was blown apart, and the bone in my leg was shattered. The shooting continued. I could not move. The bedroom blinds lay ripped open, and glass fragments covered the floor.

Searching in the Darkness

Hours later, I awoke in the intensive care unit. The sounds of beeping machines surrounded me. My right knee had pins surgically inserted into the bone. My bandaged leg hung elevated with weights attached to prevent any movement. My left arm was covered in a plaster cast. Viggo was nowhere to be found. I know Viggo didn't physically pull the trigger, but he was the catalyst behind the bullets.

I was sure God was punishing me. As I lay motionless and silent, it occurred to me that all my searching for love and acceptance had brought me to this place of hopelessness. There was no escape from the pain and suffering or the uncertainty of my future.

For the next six months, I was completely bedridden. Eventually, when my femur did not fuse together as hoped, the doctor wrapped me in a cocoon of plaster from my chest down to my ankle. The body cast would prove to be another futile attempt at fusing my shattered bones.

I was consumed with shame, fear, and anger. My family had abandoned me. Viggo left me in the hospital for the nurses to care for me. I never saw him again. I was alone and isolated from everyone and everything familiar to me.

Eventually, the doctor removed my cast. A surgeon fused the bones in my leg together using a bone fragment from my hip. A metal rod placed in my leg added strength during the healing process. My leg was now permanently two inches shorter. My injuries required the following year in intense rehabilitation therapy.

Finding Hope

When a friend invited me to attend a baptismal service at her church, I agreed to go because of the transformation I saw in her. When I heard the testimonies of other broken people, the good news of the gospel filled my heart with hope.

Recovering from the trauma of physical, emotional, and spiritual brokenness became a long journey. At times, I questioned whether I would ever reclaim wholeness again. All my efforts to start a new life had failed miserably. That night, I asked Jesus to be my Lord and Savior. I am so grateful that he had a better purpose and plan for my life.

I discovered the most devastating circumstances create an opportunity for God to reach those in the pit of despair and pull them up to higher ground. What man meant for evil, God used to provide deliverance from the destructive grip the gang held over my life. He put a new desire in my heart to follow him. I chose not to stay a victim but to be a survivor and an overcomer in God's transforming love. The Bible explains this hope: "And we know that God causes everything to work together for the good of those who love God and are called according to his purpose for them" (Romans 8:28).

I learned that deliverance and restoration come to those who open their heart to the Redeemer and Savior, Jesus Christ. He longs for each of us to have a personal encounter with the hope and healing available to us through God's transforming love. I've learned the best way to heal a broken heart is to give God all the pieces.

A lifetime of revelations waits for you to discover in God's Word.

Always remember, nothing can separate you from the love of God. You are his beloved.

Healed Body and Soul

In time, the Lord healed the bitterness and anger I held in my heart. Sin had its consequences, but his love changed my life. The Lord blessed me with a godly husband and two precious daughters. I rejoice in his provision as he prepares the path before me.

The brokenness in my life became the key that unlocked the treasures of the love I was searching for—the love of the Father. His love gave me the courage to hope, to live, and to love again. Our past does not define us. Instead, Jesus offers us a new life in him. "This means that anyone who belongs to Christ has become a new person. The old life is gone; a new life has begun!" (2 Corinthians 5:17). Imagine my joy when I discovered that the Lord loves me just as I am!

I pray that the words of my testimony will point others to the glorious hope we have in Jesus. He is our source of love. Our heavenly Father "heals the brokenhearted and bandages their wounds" (Psalm 147:3).

Renew and Restore

- When has your self-worth and sense of belonging been tested by circumstances that were out of your control?
- In what way has your brokenness become a blessing when you didn't expect it?
- 2 Corinthians 5:17 calls anyone who belongs to Christ a new person. How has your life been transformed by the God of hope and his great love?
- Describe how it feels to be restored after having been broken.

Maureen Hager is an author, inspirational speaker, and blogger. Her book, *Love's Bullet: A Wounded Victim in a Biker Gang War Transformed by God's Love*, chronicles her misguided search for love and acceptance that lured her into the life of an outlaw motorcycle gang. She suffered two gunshot wounds from M16 rifles in a violent gang war. When Maureen heard the gospel, she surrendered her heart to the Lord, and her restored life began. www.MaureenHager.com

Worn Yet Wanted

Annette Warsaw

I like worn things. Not just antiques but rusty, peeling, chippy paint and tarnish. Even with a dent or a crack, there's character and potential. For the past several years, I have shopped at a vintage market that includes hundreds of vendors peddling just these types of items. My personal favorites are windows, chairs, doors, and pieces of small furniture. Perusing the beauty in the picked over, the dirty, or worn piques my interest.

I've mucked through mud in my rain boots through spring and fall vintage markets, charged with the joy of carefully curating pretty junk for my home. My walls, shelves, and heart are full. My husband often questions the rustic items I see and fall in love with. To his surprise, sometimes I even dig through the metal and junk pile of discarded items at our farm. The more random and rusted the better.

There's a small stool on my front porch that has chipping paint, layers of history slowly peeling to reveal the smooth original wood. It sits between two reclining chairs facing the south skies here at our prairie home. My husband suggested I bring it inside because the elements will eventually wear off the paint down to the bare wood.

A sizeable old barn door painted mint green sits propped against this old brick home, bearing a large wreath and a metal star or flowers, depending on the season. Flaking paint also reveals its hundred-year-old wood. It makes me smile to know it kept out cold and wind once upon a time.

A small turquoise rusted case sits on the back step. It's a throwaway piece of junk I picked up somewhere. Stacked with random décor, it rests between flowerpots and a metal watering can. The deep hues of blueish green are peeling away to reveal a rich brown rust color. The color and depth of its details are such a contrast to the bright green buds and grass that peek in early spring.

Hidden and Worn

Yep, that's right, I like junk. Pretty junk. *Really?* you might wonder. You're not the first to question my love for the rustic. Recently when asked why I prefer "junk," I realized I see it for the beauty of the chipping paint, rust, and wear. Tossed away. Forgotten. Overlooked. But fits just perfectly in my home.

I appreciate these items for the same reason I want to be accepted. I want to be loved for who I am and not just what others see on the outside. My entire life has been a series of moving, new friends, new homes, and plenty of opportunity for a girl just wanting to fit in. It's funny how quickly I learned to put layers of protection between myself and others for fear of rejection if they saw who I really was: loud, funny, a bit crazy, and too sensitive. Even as a child, teenager, and young adult I wasn't sure how God saw me. How could anyone really know me, see me, love me for who I am?

Church was a hiding place. My father was a pastor and my mother a teacher, so my life was defined by being "on display." Protected by the pretending, layers of hiding covered me. Don't get me wrong, it isn't like I didn't stand out. I liked to perform and create all sorts of imaginative ways to appear to be more than I was. In middle school, our Bible school teacher saw me not as the pastor's daughter but as a child of God. She encouraged me to trust a God who saw me for me under all my layers. It was then I remember realizing that the beauty on the inside truly mattered. A little change began inside my heart. But challenges came, like they do.

Entering ninth grade in a new school in a much larger city soon shifted my heart a bit. Trying to fit in became harder, and my old habits of covering up my real heart returned. By the time I graduated from college, I had perfected the layering effect. Hiding in plain sight, I was not regularly attending church and was searching for purpose. Not sure who I really was. Not sure I was worthy. God had seen all that I had done in college. All my mistakes and missteps. Surely that was too much for a God I once knew well. But God knows exactly what we need even if we aren't sure.

Revealed Beauty

When I met my husband and we attended his family church, I was reminded that I had control over what I let others see about me. I tested the waters with coworkers, attended Bible study where I found my voice in faith, and slowly shifted my purpose and future closer to living out loud for Jesus. Why had I hidden it so long? Allowing others to see my cracks was always hard for fear of rejection. Somehow though, being myself in prayer or worship chipped off the tough outer layers I had so long built up in an effort to fit in. For the first time as an adult, his promise of unconditional love gave me confidence.

Little pieces of my paint peeled off. The rust started to show, and it wasn't bad. In fact, I felt better than I had expected. I have always worn my heart on my sleeve, but this was different.

I allowed myself to shine because of the unwavering love of a God that truly sees me and knows me and *still* loves me. That's impressive. My mistakes, failures, wrong words, and misguided thoughts couldn't keep me from his love. All the shabby layers of paint, rust, and junk proved to be the most beautiful ugly thing.

The God who created the earth, moon, and stars is ok with who I am. And not just ok, he *loves* me. He sees my faults and still pursues my heart. He even has a purpose for me for his glory. The elements do make a difference. But we can expect to be protected and sheltered by a God that promises to never leave us. Never. Thankfully for us as believers, we have redemption. For he promises us nothing can separate us from the love of God.

> No, despite all these things, overwhelming victory is ours through Christ, who loved us. And I am convinced that nothing can ever separate us from God's love. Neither death nor life, neither angels nor demons, neither our fears for today nor our worries about tomorrow—not even the powers of hell can separate us from God's love. No power in the sky above or in the earth below—indeed, nothing in all creation will ever be able to separate us from the love of God that is revealed in Christ Jesus our Lord. (Romans 8:37–39)

Created for a Purpose

Even our cracked, ugly layers can be used for his glory. We have beauty and purpose hiding under all of that brokenness. So many times in Scripture, God used overlooked people, often wounded, cast out, dirty, unassuming, scandalous, and hated people for his glory. In fact, I might suggest that all the stories of the Bible expose layers of less-than people. God used them to fulfill his purposes.

His strength was proven not in spite of but because of their weaknesses. Shepherds were considered lowly and dirty, but an angel came to them, and they were the first to share the message of the great Messiah's arrival. Jesus met a woman at a well who had a sordid past. Despite her past, Jesus sought her out, and she became a voice to many about a Jesus who sees us and knows our name.

In the book of Genesis, a man named Joseph, an unassuming brother cast out by his own siblings, landed in jail yet faithfully stepped into a role interpreting dreams. In leadership, he fulfilled dreams proving that faith is real. Moses couldn't speak well and questioned his abilities as a leader. He made mistakes, including murder, yet he believed God's promises and led God's people into a place of hope.

A nasty Pharisee named Saul persecuted believers in Christ, yet he saw a great light and had a run-in with Jesus on the way to a town called Damascus. He became a great preacher. We know him as Paul, a man whose words and actions fill the pages of Scripture and who shared the gospel to the early church.

These people were just like you and me. They could have been considered unworthy, but God had other plans to fulfill his purposes. In his letter to the people of Corinth, the apostle Paul—the same one mentioned above—talks about his weakness being used by God. "Three different times I begged the Lord to take it away. Each time he said, 'My grace is all you need. My power works best in weakness.' So now I am glad to boast about my weaknesses, so that the power of Christ can work through me. That's why I take pleasure in my weaknesses, and in the insults, hardships, persecutions, and troubles that I suffer for Christ. For when I am weak, then I am strong" (2 Corinthians 12:8–10).

My collection of cherished goodies with chippy paint and rust reminds me that we are all exposed to the elements of life. Rejection, tragedy, fear, and expectations wear on us. We are human and are bound to make mistakes and fail. Without a Savior who reminds us how very much we are loved and valued, we might just feel like tossed, forgotten, ugly junk too. But God made us. We are his creation, marvelous and wonderful.

"You made all the delicate, inner parts of my body and knit me together in my mother's womb. Thank you for making me so wonderfully complex! Your workmanship is marvelous—how well I know it" (Psalms 139:13–14). The creator of the world—*the world*—made you. To him, we are a cherished treasure. Beautiful and adored even with layers of chipping paint and rust.

Renew and Restore

- What kind of things do you like to collect? How does your collection represent who you are?

- Is there a part of your life, past, or personality you've wished you could hide from God? God can handle your honesty when you pray about it and tell him how you feel.
- Think about the Bible stories you know. Which person in the Bible whom God used for his good purposes do you most recognize in yourself?

Annette Warsaw is a Jesus girl, farmer's wife, and mother to a beautiful daughter. She loves to collect and create in her Illinois home. A photographer and graphic designer by trade, she adores big hugs, belts out pretty much any music she may or may not know the words to, and is obsessed with flowers, food, and a good campfire. Annette enjoys crafting motivational words and is a Scripture-reading kind of girl!

Finding Warmth After Wynter

Ree Boado

"It's not fair! Why us?!" I exploded, then fell into my husband's arms, sobbing like a child. My hands gripped desperately to his body while a chill ran through our Tennessee home, as autumn turned into winter, and winter felt like it would never end. I prayed for God to take me out of this world. I couldn't fathom how it was possible to live with a stabbing pain in my heart. "God have mercy!" I would plea, yet sometimes I wondered why I was still praying at all. God had not answered the most important prayer of my life. The one that would let my daughter live and grow up before my eyes.

We named her Wynter, though she was born on the autumn morning of October 17, 2018, the best and worst day of my life. Wynter Monet Celisa, our long-awaited breath of fresh air after eighteen years of marriage with no kids. Our little miracle. She was going to bring a new dynamic to our relationship, so when I found that the name Wynter symbolized a bringing of renewal, I knew it was perfect. It had a depth and a poetic nature that just felt right for the daughter of two creatives.

She was a full-term, healthy baby, as far as anyone knew, until she stopped breathing after forty-five minutes. Those few moments together were filled with the most overwhelming sense of love I have ever felt for another human being. Staring into those deep brown eyes, I would've died for that little half-Filipina girl in a heartbeat.

Our Wynnie-Pooh didn't look much like me, but it didn't matter. I was stunned at how her miraculous entry into our world could instantly transform me into a fierce mama bear. My heart expanded a hundred-fold to hold love for my beautiful daughter, an absolute gift from God.

The medical staff was eventually successful in resuscitating Wynter after twenty-four minutes. She was kept on life support for seven days until we had to make the decision no parent wants to make. We had to release our precious newborn daughter from our aching arms into the arms of Jesus. It was the most costly sacrifice I have ever made. I wondered how a person could ever fully recover from this. Was God, in fact, big enough to handle this nightmare of sorrow and loss? He was going to have to be.

Something New Is Birthed

Early on, my husband and I knew that we couldn't let Wynter's devastating death define us. Though we were heartbroken, we couldn't end up being "the parents who lost their only child." How depressing. We had a choice to turn away in anger or rely on God's strength to carry us through the thick clouds of grief that now hung over us. My faith, being shaken to the bone, would have to be rebuilt, as I felt so wounded by God and disappointed in his decision to not answer my prayer for Wynter's life. It took me quite some time to forgive him and learn to trust once again that he knows all things and promises to redeem *all* things.

I've always loved expressing myself through various forms of the arts. It's cathartic and healing and how I process the world. Whether it's singing, songwriting, poetry, or painting, I value these things and think of them as a way that I communicate with the Ultimate Creative.

It was no surprise that five months after losing Wynter, I started to feel God calling me to write. My story could help someone else, and the writing process would help me heal. Though I had no aspirations of becoming an author, I embarked upon writing my first book, which is now almost completed. I held tightly to this newfound belief that my raw, in-process journey back to him could bring hope to another floundering soul in search of reconnecting with Jesus and their purpose here.

During the early stages of writing, I had a steady companion of tears as I sorted through the agony churning inside. Filled with confusion and doubts about who God really was, I questioned his love and concern for people in the midst of his ultimate plans for humanity. I wanted to know the age-old question: if God is really so good, then why does he allow such horrific suffering for his people?

Not once did I sense that he was angry about my doubts. Rather, he welcomed these conversations and had great patience with me in my lack of understanding. He offered a compassionate presence, as one who also suffered and knew the sting of what I had lost. I searched the Bible to understand God's purpose for suffering, focusing on the books of Job and Lamentations. I read lots of books and stories from other loss parents who found their way back to God. These things gave me some answers and more insight into the mysterious God we seek to know. But it also left me with more questions.

What truly began to heal my heart was quietly sitting, closing my eyes, and telling God, "I receive your love and comfort. Please help me." His peace always came if I was willing to wait with him. It sounds so simple, but it isn't. It's vulnerable to receive something, especially when you don't trust the giver. You have to let your guard down and relinquish control, which is so hard after you've been ravaged by disaster.

Trusting again is *very* hard. I found that as I sat with Jesus over and over again, pouring out my soul on the page and asking for his love to be enough, my roughened, jaded heart slowly became soft again.

God was birthing something different from what I had planned, and I could follow his lead or resist it. The choice was mine, and I chose him.

Becoming a Wounded Healer

When you are confronted with something so life-altering as holding your child until they breathe their last, you don't walk away the same person.

You are pushed to examine your actions in life and the purpose of life in general. In the first several months following Wynter's death, I felt a strong pull to make my daughter's short existence matter. To do something in this world to make her proud or make my life feel significant. What we do does not create our worth in the eyes of God. But filled with grief, there was a desire to see that grief bring forth something of beauty.

I had allowed fear to hold me back from nudges from God in the past, but after losing my baby girl, I didn't want to live life that way anymore. God was suddenly enabling me to look outward and live boldly. To see all his children that he loved dearly, as much as I loved Wynter.

Five months later, I walked into the local jail as a mentor.

I volunteered at the jail for a few months and met with one woman we'll call Angel. She was loud and hilarious, with a lifetime of trauma. She and I bonded over being separated from our daughters. We laughed, cried, and talked about our dysfunctional childhoods, losses, and the hope we were both finding in Jesus. Somehow, I left encouraged every time by showing up for someone in my brokenness. God used those conversations to mend something within us both.

As God walked with my husband and me, we continued to grieve forward. Eight months after Wynter went to heaven, we welcomed a hurting fifteen-year-old girl into our home to foster. One month later, a twelve-year-old girl joined our makeshift family.

Fostering the girls for nine months was one of the most beautiful yet difficult growth experiences. We struggled and made mistakes, but God repeatedly gave us energy to love them in spite of their challenging trauma effects. Through fostering children, the Lord allowed us to be a part of helping others heal, even when we ourselves were still in the messy process of being healed.

All of us had experienced grief, loss, and separation from family, and yet a glimmer of redemption was taking place because of our willingness to be uncomfortable. And when the time came for both of them to be reunited with their own mothers, we were grateful to have been part of their lives and recovery.

Though wounded ourselves, God gave us the courage to love on two girls who desperately needed parents. It wasn't about our abilities. It was about relying on his strength and wisdom, despite our many weaknesses.

God, in his incredible love for humanity, can take the most tragic and life-shattering events of our lives and use them for healing in ways we could never imagine. We are intricately connected as humans, and our suffering is often a building block for someone else's restoration.

Surrendering Longings

Life is filled with intense longings. We strive and fight to get to the thing we believe will fill us with joy once and for all and finally remove our pain. Even still, there is a part of us that knows that our deepest yearnings can never fully be satisfied by the love of another person, a purposeful career, or the family we hoped for.

More than two years later, I still ache for my daughter, and I pray I can birth another child. So far, this has not been God's plan, but I'm choosing to believe life can still be meaningful, even when it's not the life we expected. God has healed others through our despair, which is teaching me to trust that he is legitimately capable of redeeming *all* things.

As I sit with him and receive his love, I am discovering that it's safe to release my desires into his care. This verse has become real to me: "For he satisfies the thirsty and fills the hungry with good things" (Psalm 107:9).

Surrendering my sincere longing for a child is not a simple undertaking. It requires daily persistence. Handing over anything we passionately desire to see fulfilled in this life requires trust.

Trust in God only comes by knowing his unconditional, expansive love for us. Knowing his love comes by humbly asking and receiving it, which comes by being vulnerable enough to need it more than anything else this life can offer.

Renew and Restore

- Think about the main desire you know you need to surrender into God's hands. What fear is keeping you from trusting him with it?
- When you're ready to release the fear, imagine placing this desire safely into a box and handing it over to Jesus. Have grace on yourself and receive his peace and love today. He is ever patient and gentle with us.
- Where has God used your heartbreak to provide hope or healing for someone else? Consider one possible way you could strengthen others on a similar path.

Ree Boado has been pursuing inner healing for over twenty years. Having shared about hope after childhood trauma with various nonprofits through songs and art, Ree is now currently writing her first book about trusting God through tragedy. As a volunteer with child loss organizations, former foster parent, and vocal coach by trade, Ree is a natural born encourager. She and her husband presently live in Dundee, Scotland, with their two fur babies. www.reeboado.com

From a Place of Hurt to a Place of Blessing

Meg Glesener

Behind a closed door, huddled on a bed, comforting my young siblings, we could hear the lyric "*O Tannenbaum, O Tannenbaum*" interspersed with the louder angry yelling voices of Fred and Jeanne. That is my only memory of my parents together. Their marriage was loveless from the beginning, and from my earliest moments, my home was a place of hurt. Yelling turned to abuse.

My dad turned to alcohol and my mom went internal. When I was five, they divorced. So began a fractured decade of broken relationships and countless schools, all of us kids bouncing back and forth between households.

When you look at what is now called an ACE Score (a child's Adverse Childhood Experiences), the higher the score, the greater the likelihood of continuing the generational pattern of abuse, risky behaviors, mental issues, and health problems. My score was an eight out of ten. And I was just a little girl. Though this was not the start in life anyone would choose for their daughter, it was "normal" to me. I just coped on my own, on the inside, never really sharing my thoughts with anyone.

Insecure and Alone

When I entered high school, I was very insecure. I looked for affirmation from friends, from boys, and from my coaches. My dad would come to my games, but his alcohol consumption and anger made life very difficult, especially at home. My teen sister, brother, and I were regularly fearful, walking on eggshells. Even more stressful for us kids, my dad and step-mom had a tumultuous relationship. One night, my father's fifteen years of raging alcoholism came to a head, which included him locking himself in a room with a harpoon, a desperate drive, and him admitting himself into a clinic. A new day dawned—kind of.

My dad was now sober, but his habits of anger and demeaning were still there. So, I tried to stay out of his way and deal with all of the high school struggles alone. On the surface at school, someone may have thought I had it all. I was pretty, a good student, gaining popularity for being MVP on my sports teams, and even hanging out with the popular girls. However, I was miserable, and never felt that I belonged.

One of my friends invited me to a party in our junior year. Lance, someone I didn't know, opened his Bible and began to talk about God and wonderful things I hadn't heard before. He shared John 3:16 and told us about God's love and forgiveness. How bold was that?!

Inside my heart, I could feel something stirring. What he was sharing sounded too good to be true—that Jesus loves me, that he laid down his life for me, that I might "get saved," and one day be with him in heaven. *What is heaven anyway?* I thought.

He then asked if anyone wanted to give their life to the Lord. My heart was burning inside, and I said "Yes, I do." We bowed our heads, and I repeated with all of my heart the words he said aloud, asking Jesus to come into my heart.

A New Day Dawns

The next day when I woke up, deep in my heart I could sense a change. A burden was lifted, and there was a warmth in my soul. Excited, I found my dad and said, "What do you think about God?"

His demeanor shifted to anger and intimidation as he shared his thoughts. He made it very clear. "There is no room for God in my house."

So, I didn't tell him I was a Christian. I was too scared. I quietly finished my high school years.

In college at CSUF two years later, I began to read that Bible more often and soak up the great stories and encouraging psalms. If I heard my dad walk by my room, I would quickly hide my Bible under the covers. A friend from Bible study invited me to church, and I knew I needed to ask my dad about it.

He was very stern and angry when I asked him, but I finally had the courage to tell him I was a Christian. He said that he would rather I was on drugs than be a Christian. Christianity was a bunch of propaganda and BS. The bottom line: I could go to church once, but if I wanted to go again, I would not be welcome to stay in his home.

Well, I went to church and loved it. Are you kidding me? A whole room of people singing and freely enjoying hearing a message was such a treat. How could I keep hiding my Bible?

So, I decided to tell him. My stepmother and he sat down, sternly looking at me. When I told them that I wanted to go back to church, my dad said, "You know what that means, don't you?"

"Yes," I said, meekly.

"When are you leaving?" he said.

Fighting back tears, and stuttering, "Um . . . I don't know."

My stepmother looked coldly into my eyes, "That's not good enough, Meg, we want a date."

It was a Monday, and I said, "Wednesday."

They wouldn't let me say goodbye to my sisters, and I moved back in with my mom.

But I was free. Free to worship. Free to read. Free to be discipled. Free to grow. Free to go to church.

That same year, my mother was having some difficulty in life and spent some time in a clinic. And I moved in with a family from my church. Seeing a couple enjoy each other and talk sweetly to their kids was a gift and a place of healing for me. I was accepted and didn't need to prove anything. And that year, I met my husband, Mike.

The Difference Love Makes

Being married to a loving and kind Minnesota farm boy has been one of the greatest blessings of my life. Sometimes, people say our personal relationship with God reflects our relationship with our earthly father. I had to learn that God wasn't always mad at me and ready to pounce, but he is in fact, loving, welcoming, and forgiving.

It was a process, but slowly, insecurity was replaced with acceptance, and fear was replaced with trust. And all of that learning spilled over into our parenting, which was needed as our family grew year by year.

Definitely, some of the patterns from my childhood were struggles that I faced, especially with our first decade of parenting including a tendency toward impatience, yelling, and frustration. This is something I would pray about regularly. I read good parenting books to help renew my thinking and practiced asking forgiveness for my missteps. Over time, we were able to foster and establish a tone of love and grace in our home.

One of the core prayers in our marriage, from the day Mike proposed, is now written in our mission statement on our living room wall to remind us: "Our Home, a Place of Blessing." And there is always room for more.

Through the years, we have had many live with us—most recently, Grandpa Freddy. Yes, my dad. We gladly welcomed him in, as he had fallen on hard times. Living in our home, within just twenty-four hours, his demeanor softened. Seeing our sweet teens look at his face, with a smile, enjoying conversations, and feeling accepted melted him. Maybe he just needed more of that growing up. Life isn't easy, but change is possible, and there is always hope. For that I am grateful.

Growing up, my home was a place of hurt, and now, we are experiencing our decades of home being a place of learning, healing, and blessing. All are welcome. Home.

Renew and Restore

- How would you describe your home life growing up?
- What lingering dysfunction have you had to revisit at as an adult?
- What did you learn from your parents—good or bad?
- What change are you seeking to create in your own family as you break generational cycles?

Meg Glesener is the host and producer of the *Letters From Home* podcast, where she publishes every other week for your encouragement, "Everyday Extraordinary Faith Stories." Her podcast can be found on Spotify, Amazon, Stitcher, and all of the places podcasts live, including most social media platforms. She and her husband, Mike, and their youngest three kids live and serve in Seattle, Washington. lettersfromhomepodcast.com

See Them With Your Heart

Kolleen Lucariello

Six hours. The clock reflected the time our family had been traveling from our home in Upstate New York to my sister-in-law's home in New Jersey. We'd been invited for a surprise birthday celebration for our brother-in-law, and most of my husband's family planned to travel from different parts of the East Coast to attend. Having all of the family together was a rare event, and our children were eager to spend time with their cousins.

I didn't share in their excitement for many reasons. The preparation and packing for a family of five, the long car ride, and the anxiety of spending days with my in-laws were almost overwhelming. The in-laws and I—well, we had a history.

This particular event came on the heels of several years' worth of unresolved grievances I had held against my father-in-law. I'd already decided that this get-together would bring more of the typical irritations, hurtful comments, and demands I had become accustomed to from previous gatherings. I was not happy my husband's vacation time would be swallowed up by this trip. So, to make sure he was aware of my displeasure, I'd spent the nearly six-hour ride expressing my dissatisfaction. (There were no ear buds back in those days, friends.)

"This is our vacation time! Your father will not be calling the shots for our family," I said.

"We will spend our time doing *what WE want*, regardless of what your dad has to say," I said.

"I am not budging on this. I will not allow your father to guilt us into anything," I said.

"You'd better stand up to your dad," I said.

On and on I spouted. For six long hours I spouted—and pouted.

Oh, No! She's About to Blow!

We arrived to happy reunions with cousins who'd been missing one another, sibling hugs, and "How have you been?" Much of the first evening held laughter and conversation, games, and good food, along with the occasional insult and irritation.

The next day held all of the drama I anticipated when my father-in-law let the family know what *his* plans were for that day. The family understood what he actually meant was his plans—*for everyone*. I still recall—quite vividly, I might add—the look that pasted itself across my face in that moment. It was a look of challenge.

I gave a warning glare to my husband that said, "You'd better speak up before I do."

When his voice of explanation for our day was discounted, mine took over. "We have made plans, thank you. We will not be joining you."

The words rolled off my tongue in controlled anger as the silence in the room became palpable. I called out to our kids, asked them to get their shoes on, and to get moving. I seethed with resentment as the kids complained about leaving their cousins behind.

Wisdom Speaks Through a Child

Descending the stairs from the kitchen to our car, I allowed the anger and aggravation I was feeling to escape unfiltered through my lips. Following close behind me, my oldest son tapped my shoulder and said, "Mom," but

I ignored him. Again, he said, "Mom." Then, he too, allowed words to proceed from his mouth that would forever change my life.

Reaching out and taking hold of my shoulder, he stopped me. As I turned to face him on the stairs he said, "Mom! What are you so mad at Grandpa for?"

Responding honestly, I said, "I am mad at him for a lot of things, but right now I am mad that he is always telling us what to do."

That's when he looked me straight in the eye and said, "Mom, you can't look at Grandpa with your eyes. You need to see him with your heart."

Ouch. I felt the wind had been knocked right out of me. Or perhaps it was pride.

In that instant I knew God had used my eight-year-old son to reprimand me for my attitude. He'd also challenged a mindset I'd embraced for a very long time. As we made our way to the car his words replayed *. . . don't see Grandpa with your eyes, see him with your heart*, and I realized the negative lens I'd been using for what seemed a lifetime had just been adjusted.

Jesus Vision

In the book of Acts in the Bible, there is a story about a man named Saul and his encounter with Jesus that altered his perspective and completely changed his life. Saul had been a strong advocate for the law of Moses (Old Testament law), and because of his experiences, opinions, and beliefs, it was his understanding that the law was the only way by which someone should live. Sound familiar? This caused him to oppose anyone who believed in Jesus. Even if it meant their death. That is, until the day Jesus met him on the road.

Saul was held hostage by his own agenda and determined his way was the right way. So determined, in fact, that he gathered letters from the high priest and began a journey to Damascus with the intention of imprisoning any Jesus followers he found along the way. However, Jesus interrupted his travel plans and revealed himself to Saul as a flash of light from heaven.

When the conversation was over, Saul was left without his physical vision, but he had perfect spiritual vision for what God had planned for him. After the three days of blindness, "Instantly something like scales fell from Saul's eyes, and he regained his sight" (Acts 9:18). Saul had been consumed by inaccuracies about Jesus until the truth of Jesus confronted him.

We are no different. It's easy to become consumed by inaccuracies about others unless we experience an encounter with Jesus that gives us our sight back, too.

So Long, Resentment

Jesus interrupted my travel plans in a garage in New Jersey. I was on the Road of Resentment that led to a destination of division and dysfunction. I had been tying an imaginary string around my fingers in an effort to remember every account of wrong against me. I had rehearsed them so as to not forget a single one. Then, when given a new opportunity to be offended, I would simply add that to the list.

The Lord had just blown that habit up by revealing to me that regardless of every justifiable reason ever given me to be hurt or mad, I was now the one held hostage to anger and resentment. I needed to be set free from this life of constant turmoil, and through the wisdom of an eight-year-old, God had just given me instruction on how to begin the process.

My first act of freedom was repentance. For many years, I allowed myself to react rather than give a thoughtful response when hit by inconsideration or wounded by words. He reminded me that I had a relationship with Jesus. My father in-law did not. Therefore, because my identity is found in Christ and not in the opinions of others, I am able to respond in a manner similar to how Jesus did—in love.

I moved into another place of freedom by realizing God was offering me the ability to see beyond the outward appearance to peek deeper into a man's heart. It is often said, "hurting people hurt people," and once I was able to hear words spoken from a hurting heart, I was able to disengage quicker from the conflict.

Freedom is found when we relinquish our right to hold so tightly to a mindset based solely upon what is happening in the here and now, and instead, develop a mindset like Jesus's through the study of God's Word.

When annoyances arise, someone needs to make the first move at reconciliation and change the music if the dance is to change. God spoke to my heart and said that it would need to be me. I was going to learn the art of forgiving. I would be challenged to refuse every invitation to be offended and learn how to love others. Unconditionally—just like Jesus.

There hasn't been much that's changed in my relationship with my father in-law, but a great deal of transformation has happened within me. I gave up my rights to be right and prove a point because I no longer see him through my eyes. I see him through God's.

I am convinced that, like Saul, Jesus removed the scales from my eyes on the steps that day. He used my son to begin the process of changing an old negative mindset. Never assume God can't use children to speak truth to us. He sure can, and he will. We simply need to have our spiritual ears open to hear what he's trying to tell us. When we do, we will discover the joy of a new identity—a true identity—that is found only in Christ.

Review and Restore

- We can become experts at tying invisible strings around each finger to help us replay and remember insult or hurt. Satan uses this tactic to bring division through grudges and resentment. How will you choose to let go of insults and injuries that you've "remembered" for too long?
- Instead of resorting to quick snarky comebacks or the silent treatment (only to bust open once alone with a friend or spouse), what actions demonstrate the art of responding thoughtfully rather than reacting?
- Proverbs 19:11 says, "Sensible people control their temper; they earn respect by overlooking wrongs." Whose wrongs have irritated you? Are you willing to practice overlooking them?

Kolleen Lucariello is the author of *#beYOU: Change Your Identity One Letter at a Time.* She is Co-Executive Director of Activ8Her, Inc., a ministry passionate about helping women activ8 a personal relationship in Christ and then live empowered from their identity in Christ. She and her husband, Pat, make their home in Upstate New York. She is the mother of three married kids and Mimi to six beautiful grands. Get to know her at www.speakkolleen.com

Requalified By Grace

Teresa Janzen

My *heart sank as my* pastor delivered the news. "We've decided to hire someone else for the position of church secretary." Recently divorced and a single parent, I knew it would be hard to find a job. The advertised position for part-time secretary in my hometown community church seemed my best chance. This rejection was further evidence I was disqualified for ministry. Now what was I going to do? Even the church did not want me.

"But I think I know an option that might be even better," he continued. *Even better?* The words echoed without meaning in my head. *How could anything be better?* The church was the only place I could think of with the flexibility and grace I needed to work and care for my four young children. I gave the pastor permission to forward my resume to whomever he wanted. Then I sank to floor and hung up the phone.

Maybe it was a mistake to return home following the divorce. But where else could I go? I had no savings and no job. My mom helped me buy a small house just down the road from where I grew up. I enrolled the older girls in school. The buildings looked the same, only smaller. My daughter Kelly was even assigned the same fourth grade teacher I had many years before. That Sunday, my oldest daughter was stopped in the Sunday school hallway, "Are you Teresa's daughter?" a woman inquired.

Indeed, there is no denying the similarities we share. It was nice to be somewhere familiar, but maybe it was too familiar.

A Promising Start

Church had been an integral part of my life growing up, and I loved every part of it. If the church doors were open, our family was there. It was entirely possible we were such faithful attendees to give my mom, also a single parent of four rambunctious kids, a needed break from time to time. Regardless of the motives, I loved it and longed for one more sticker on my memory verse chart and a leading role in the Sunday school play.

I didn't know it at the time, but the church also contributed financially to my spiritual formation. Every summer, we were sent to youth camp—on scholarship. It was the summer I turned fifteen when a guest speaker, a missionary from Saudi Arabia, gave an altar call that changed the course of my life. Blood rushed to my head and my heart pounded. Muffled voices all around me sang, *"just as I am . . . I come."* I rushed past my camp cohorts, dropped to my knees at the altar, and dedicated my life to serving God on the foreign mission field. Later that night, tucked into my sleeping bag, I cried myself to sleep with one thought in mind. *No one will ever marry me if I become a missionary.*

While I had not dated much in high school, college presented a whole new opportunity for socializing. Boys at the small Bible college liked girls with a heart for ministry—girls like me. Relieved that I may not be sentenced to a life of singleness, I began interviewing possible candidates to partner with in my vocation as a missionary.

During the summer, I worked as a late-night waitress at a restaurant frequented by local guys. One such regular, quite a flirt and a good tipper, asked me if I wanted to go for a ride on his motorcycle and watch the sunrise. That first ride was a fitting metaphor for the next few months—fast and dangerous.

Damaged Goods

Small-town girls from Bible colleges should not date older, motorcycle-riding, local guys. It was not long before the relationship turned physical, and I considered myself married in the biblical sense. He began to be more controlling, wanting to know where I was all the time and dictating my friendships and clothing style. But what was I to do? I had made my bed—or rather, slept in his—so now I had to face the consequences. It was here that I realized I may once again wind up single and alone unless this guy asked me to be his wife. Shortly after he proposed, I found out I was pregnant.

The night before our wedding, as I prepared for the rehearsal, my mom fixed my hair and said matter-of-factly, "You don't have to go through with this."

What did she know? Had she noticed the warning signs I tried to ignore?

My heart screamed, *You don't understand! Yes, I do.* I struggled to hold back tears and replied, "I know."

I dropped out of college to raise our daughter. Soon a second was on the way. The missionary life I thought God had called me to seemed far away. I homeschooled the girls and participated in church activities, but I had few friendships. If I went out on my own, I would risk inciting his jealousy. A few years later, a third daughter was added.

At times I thought I was losing my mind. He controlled every aspect of my life—or tried to. I experimented with various coping mechanisms: anorexia, alcohol, and eventually an affair. Anything to try and take some-thing back for myself. As I asserted my independence, he sought compan-ionship with a female colleague. To squelch the growing rumors about the state of our marriage, we decided to add baby number four to our brood.

Reprieve

Daughter number four arrived with the happiest baby disposition imag-inable. I felt as if God knew I was at the end of my rope, so he sent me a chubby, bald angel to help me hold on. My husband's interests continued toward his young colleague, so I told him it was time to make a choice.

While I had endured years of mental and emotional oppression, his unrepentant unfaithfulness provided what appeared to me as biblically legitimate grounds for divorce.

Moving back home, I found myself free in some ways, but I was still bound with feelings of guilt, shame, failure, and unworthiness. I had completely messed up God's plan for my life, and now I must make do with what surely must be God's plan B for me. *Clearly, I am no longer qualified to be a missionary,* I thought. Now it appeared I was disqualified from being a church secretary as well.

Requalified

My pastor's recommendation led to an interview with a local faith-based, non-profit organization providing mentoring services to at-risk youth. It was part-time, flexible, and exciting work. I stood before the board of directors and shared not only my qualifications but also the general circumstances that led to my status as a divorced Christian.

The very idea of a divorced Christian seems an oxymoron to many people. After all, marriage is one of the holy sacraments and an analogy for our relationship with God. While Scripture does address the issue of divorce in various circumstances, people still struggle with whether God allows divorce and under what circumstances.

If we think about divorce in the context of allowable circumstances, we are missing the point completely. Trying to legitimize certain circumstances for divorce is like trying to give an excuse for any other broken or sinful behavior. Divorce, like every form of brokenness, grieves the heart of God and has serious consequences for all people involved (including children).

Relationships can be broken inside and outside the framework of marriage. It is not the act of divorce that makes a relationship displeasing to God. Abusive, controlling, manipulative, selfish, and prideful marriage relationships are just as grievous and fail to reflect God's beautiful design for marriage.

Over the years since my divorce, God revealed to me my own sin and brokenness within my first marriage. Guilt and shame may indicate a need for repentance, which brings about forgiveness and restoration. But if guilt and shame continue after sincere repentance, we may be listening to lies from the Enemy or pridefully refusing God's grace.

God never intended for me to suffer in my marriage nor to cause suffering to others. He used that first job interview as an introduction to his grace and restoration. When I was hired as the executive director of that small ministry, I began to understand that divorce is not the unforgivable sin. Jesus's death and resurrection paid the price for all my sin—past, present, and future—and he invites me to repentance and restoration.

Today I serve in ministry on the foreign mission field with my husband, Dan. Over the years, I have had to give an account of my divorce and remarriage to many boards and agencies. That is just the way things are for people in ministry. Some people may listen to my story with judgment, but most respond with grace. With Dan's support, I was able to return to college and complete my bachelor's degree and then continue for a master's in education.

My long and crooked journey to the mission field has scars from the choices and detours I took along the way. But God has healed my broken heart and brought me to a closer relationship with him. Today, he uses my scars to point others to hope and restoration.

Renew and Restore

- Are you suffering from guilt and shame because of unrepented brokenness? God is ready to listen and offer forgiveness and grace. Take a moment to talk to him.
- Describe your experience with feeling disqualified because of something from your past. How did you emotionally heal?

- After repenting of sin, are you hanging on to any shame that prevents you from experiencing God's restoration? Write a journal entry about how you release that shame, then write a statement about what you know to be true about how God sees you.
- Are you willing to allow God to use your story of brokenness to bring someone else to restoration? Where do you think he will use you first?

Teresa Janzen—writer, speaker, and teacher. She engages big issues and extends an invitation to thoughtful dialogue. Her experience in non-profit administration and global ministry ignites a passion for missional living and drives her to share stories, inspiring people to action, joy, and gratitude. Teresa is married to Dan, and together they serve as missionaries in South Sudan. They have a blended family of eight adult children and eleven grandchildren. Connect with Teresa at www.teresajanzen.com.

Interrupted Plans and a Bypassed Blowup

Betty Predmore

Vacations. *We plan. We ponder. We pack.* We strive for perfection. At least, I hope I am not the only one who approaches vacations this way. Many of us save all year for this memory-making trip and we have such high expectations. Such was the case on my vacation several years ago.

We had planned a two-week camping trip to the Central California coast. Our van was packed, our luggage rack was loaded with tents, including a three-room tent for sleeping, a large tent for eating and playing, and a shower tent. My husband is the king of camping, and we had it all. We looked like a commercial for Bass Pro Shop!

Of course, being a mom and an over-planner, I had a long list of necessities that should accompany us on our trip. (Can anybody say "control freak"?) My poor husband tried to fit all of these "necessities" and ended up having to add a small tow rack to the hitch on our van. There he loaded our bags and suitcases and tied them with rope. I took a picture of our van the night before we left and aptly tagged it on social media as "everything but the kitchen sink."

My kids think part of the great adventure of a road trip is to leave in the wee hours before the sun comes up. So off we went, with the sun still sleeping, ready for our eight-hour drive. As we started off, I did what any self-respecting, overworked, exhausted mother would do. I fell asleep. (I know I am not the only one who does this, so I refuse to feel guilty for it.)

Interrupted Bliss

About an hour into our trip, just as the sun was peeking out, my husband woke me. Apparently, the car behind us had passed us and honked, so my husband pulled over to see what the problem was.

He got out of the car, walked around the back, and then came to my side of the car with five words no woman wants to hear on day one of vacation, "Honey, we have a problem."

I got out and went around to the back of the car, and to my surprise, several of our bags were dragging along behind the car. Obviously, the rope had come untied and the bags had been dragging for a while because several of them had highway abrasions. And the clothing in those areas had been shredded.

To say the least, I was extremely frustrated and started gathering up the bags and throwing them into the van—the one with four kids. (Did I mention that the van was already stuffed to the gills, and the kids barely had breathing room?)

As I was tossing the bags into the van, I realized that I didn't see the red suitcase that held the grownup clothes. We looked around and there was no sign of the suitcase. So, we put our two brilliant minds together and came to the conclusion that our suitcase had to be further back down the road. (We are extra special in the genius department when on vacation.)

We turned around and headed in the direction from which we had come. A short way back, I spotted a red suitcase sitting in the middle of the highway. Overjoyed with the fact that I had found my clothing, I had my husband turn around and pull to the side of the road so I could retrieve our suitcase.

I jumped out of the car and ran out to the center of the road, intent on getting my belongings and getting back on our way. Much to my surprise, and not in a good way, the suitcase was totally empty—with the exception of one pair of my pink underwear that was hanging proudly from the bent metal frame of my suitcase.

I don't know about you, but having my undies waving on the highway is not a "plus" for me! In frustration and anger, I picked up that suitcase and I hurled it to the side of the road.

How often in our anger do we toss relationships or opportunities to the side, discarding them because of the emotion of the moment?

Since the suitcase was virtually empty, once again my husband and I put our brilliant minds together and determined that if our suitcase was empty, then our clothes must be yet even further back on the highway. (Are you recognizing this pattern of intelligence that is forming?) So, we turned around again and headed back toward home.

Backtracking Detour

Just a short way down the highway, we saw what I now dub as "the catastrophe on the highway." Our clothes were scattered all over the thoroughfare and cars were driving over our belongings. We turned around and pulled to the side of the road and got out to pick up as much of our clothing as we could.

If you have ever bent down to pick up a piece of paper only to have the wind blow it away from you at the last moment, then you know exactly how we felt. I can now positively assure you that the same thing happens to your undergarments when they are spread across lanes of traffic. Cars were honking at us, our clothes flying, and I was getting madder by the moment.

I grabbed up as much as I could, with my husband doing the same, and we threw it in the van. I was so angry that I could feel the steam rising off me. Vacation was ruined! After all the planning and preparation, now this? My husband got in the driver's seat as I threw the last of the clothes into the van, covering my poor kids with my belongings.

I hurled open my door and flung myself down on the seat. I turned and looked at my children and saw that they were all staring at me, eyes wide and mouths open, waiting to see what my response would be. I glanced over at my husband and his face was much the same. No one even appeared to be breathing in that moment of silence (and probably fear).

In that moment, the Lord spoke to me.

As clearly as if he were sitting in the seat next to me, I heard him say, "The way you respond in this moment will make or break your vacation."

I realized the responsibility I had at that moment and how my anger could affect the outcome. I had a choice to make. Would this ruin our vacation and send us home? Or would we make the best of the situation and proceed with our plans? It was all up to me.

The Responsibility Is Ours

As mothers, we have so much power over the hearts of our family and over circumstances and situations. Our attitudes can define our families. "A wise woman builds her home, but a foolish woman tears it down with her own hands" (Proverbs 14:1). This is a great reminder to us.

So, in that moment, with my family waiting in dreaded anticipation, I decided to do the opposite of what my family expected me to do. I chose to veer off my usual path of anger and frustration, a piece of myself I have battled with most of my life. I decided to burst out laughing. (Those who know me know this is not my normal response. But when the Lord speaks to you, you need to listen.)

When I started to laugh, they all sighed in relief. We could literally feel the weight being released from the car. And as I laughed, they joined in.

We spent the next several hours laughing about our situation. When we got to our destination that day, we had to do a little shopping. But we replaced what was damaged and went on to have one of the most beautiful vacations we have ever experienced.

That day anger did not win. That day the devil was not able to ruin our plans. That day joy triumphed over anger. That day, God got my attention.

God opened my eyes to something that has been a constant struggle in my life. He helped me realize I have the power to overcome my anger, and I have the power to choose how I respond in negative situations. That experience brought me the confidence to know I am capable of making a change. "For I can do everything through Christ, who gives me strength" (Philippians 4:13).

Renew and Restore

- Think about a time when your well-laid plans have been interrupted. How did you respond in that moment?
- Has there been a time in your life when you have felt as if God were sitting on your shoulder and whispering in your ear? How did you respond?
- Consider how you react in anger. Are there certain words, actions, or situations that set you off? By identifying those triggers, what will you do to change your reaction to something different?

Betty Predmore is an author, speaker, and ministry leader who enjoys connecting with and loving on women through the love of Jesus and the beautiful Word of God. She is a wife and a mother of seven darlings, including biological and adopted children. Her ministry, Mom-Sense, Inc. reaches women across the country with a motto of Mentorship, Connection & Service. You can visit her a www.momsenseinc.org or www.bettypredmore.com.

Use Me Broken

Kathy Carlton Willis

I *find myself gravitating toward used* furniture, thrift store finds, and resale stores. I wasn't always that way. After we bought our first home, we had a brand-new cherry Queen Anne dining room set. It was my proud possession (maybe too proud?). We enjoyed hosting dinner parties. Imagine my dismay when an unhappy child fisted his silverware upright and pounded it on the table until the veneer chipped.

Then a cold punch bowl contrasted with the heat of a sunbeam, causing the veneer to bubble up. I found out that even solid wood furniture is often finished with veneer tops to get that neat grain pattern we admire. It was an early life lesson to place less importance on possessions because people are more valuable than things. Having dinner with that young family mattered, not having pristine furniture.

Now I gravitate toward used items that have extra personality or evoke special memories. A few more scratches just add character. When guests come into our home, they comment that it's so welcoming and relaxing—the thrift store finds remind them of a more peaceful time in their lives. It's like going to Grandma's house and unplugging from a busy life to enjoy a moment of comfy-cozy calm. I'm glad they feel that way. (Of course, my husband teases me and says it looks like old people live here—and *we're* the old people! I take exception to that.)

Qualified Because of Loss

I suppose my life is like that used-but-useful furniture. I've had a number of trials hit that left me wounded and weary. I was born with a condition that caused me to not be able to bear children. Five adoption attempts fell through as well.

Circumstances forced us to have a living estate sale, not once in our lives but twice, as we let go of 75 percent of what we owned in order to walk away from a closed door while waiting for another door to open. Having answered prayers on pause with possessions whittled down is difficult for anyone to endure.

God provided in ways we could not have imagined, let alone pray for. This resulted in frequent moves to new states and towns. Each time, God helped us figure out how to start over and gave us new friends.

Have you ever noticed that trials don't come one at a time but seem to hit some people in multiples? One way I cope is to employ humor. It has a way of making my heart grin. So, when I think about accumulating trials, I say I'm adding to my collection. What is in *your* collection of scratch-and-dent situations?

I seem to have an endless supply of health trials, too. Besides acquiring a list of chronic conditions, I've had over twenty surgeries, hundreds of medications, doctors, and tests. This is one stash I'd hate to see anyone collect.

Used Goods Get Used by God

One thing I wrestled with early in this life of loss is the question: "Where is God in this?" I believed he could heal, he could provide, he could make things reverse back to the way things were. But he chose not to. I asked him why, and very clearly it seemed he gave me the answer. "I plan to use you broken."

It took the pressure off me. I wasn't a Queen Anne cherry dining set. I was a thrift store find. I'm a broken person helping other broken people.

Now, don't get me wrong. God healed me where it mattered—my soul. Such joy! Such peace! Such hope! I learned my circumstances didn't have to get better to sense God's presence. And when all else is stripped away, God's *enoughness* is truly sufficient. Talk about having a new, minimalistic perspective on life!

Show Me Your Scars

I'll never forget the summer I served as camp counselor for junior and senior high students. As I packed to get ready to go, I realized I would be getting dressed in front of these girls. Not much privacy in those cabins. All of a sudden, a new feeling emerged—dread. Would my surgical scars repulse them? I have twenty-two visible disfiguring scars. More that are hidden. If I expected these girls to get real with me, I had to risk getting real with them. This was another time for God to use me broken.

I decided to come clean with them the first night and give a devotion on the topic of scars. All of us have them. Some are just more apparent than others. God used that time of letting down my guard to share my heart. One by one, the girls opened up to me and to each other. God met us in that circle as we surrendered our pride and our painful scars to him.

I find myself gravitating toward music that speaks of brokenness and wounds. Not only do the melodies draw me in, but I can tell by the lyrics that those songwriters get me. They understand what it means to live life flawed. As I read about their lives, I uncover stories of loss and triumph. One artist underwent vocal cord surgery and had to be silent for two months of recovery. Can you imagine being a singer, not knowing if you would ever sing again? I had a similar trial when I had thyroid cancer surgery and lost one octave of my singing voice range. Oh, how I miss that part of my worship!

Grace Your Grief

Loss of any kind is hard. It stinks. It's okay to mourn and grieve, even if others think we should buck up and get over it. I've learned through back-to-back-to-back losses that I have to grace my grief. (And if I won't, who will?)

Counselors talk about the five stages of grief. I think I have the five hundred revolving doors of grief! Believers aren't exempt from pain and loss, but we do have a partner who never leaves us to deal with it alone. The Bible talks about joining in the fellowship of Christ's suffering. Not a club anyone wants to be a part of, but if we have to be in it, it's good to have a Savior who has experienced life trials to hold our hands.

The Overs of Whelming

I'm so over being overwhelmed, aren't you? I know what *over* means, but what does *whelmed* mean, anyway? All I know is the "overs of whelming" is not the kind of overachieving I want in my life! But it does help me recognize when my stress levels are getting heaven high. I don't want my stress to get to my afterlife destination before I do. Although they might land there at the same time if I don't handle being broken better.

Don't get me wrong—I can't wait to see Jesus, but not if it causes me to miss out on any opportunities he has for me here. I've learned personal stewardship means managing my time and stress better. Being broken doesn't earn me a get-out-of-jail-free card. I still have to take care of myself.

Sometimes God lightens my burdens. It's like he knows I can't take any more stress (of course he knows!). He whooshes in and clears the burdens off my back, one by one. Color me grateful for this relief. There are some stresses that he allows to be chronic (and not all of them are health related). For many of us, chronic relationship issues feel like they will break us. Even if the situations don't change, having God lighten the weight of it helps.

It all boils down to this. If remaining broken brings him big glory, I'm all in. It's all for God's glory and others' good. God makes sure my good is taken care of as well. One way God does this is to infuse my soul with joy. Joy is like a grin on the inside!

What blows me away is how Jesus found joy enduring suffering. If he can, we can too. "We do this by keeping our eyes on Jesus, the champion who initiates and perfects our faith. Because of the joy awaiting him, he endured the cross, disregarding its shame. Now he is seated in the place of honor beside God's throne" (Hebrews 12:2).

God wants to use me broken, but he restored my soul.

Renew and Restore

- What area of your life is broken? What has been your hardest struggle with it?
- Tell of a time someone made a difference in your life because they had suffered brokenness and from that experience knew how to reach out to you.
- How might you help others because of what you've gone through in life?
- Creative activity idea: take a jaunt around Pinterest or your favorite thrift or antique store. Find the potential use for items that have a little wear on them. Brainstorm ways to transform them to serve a brand-new purpose. Imagine where you'd place them in your home for décor or function. As you're doing this exercise, ask God to show you how he is using you despite your flaws and brokenness. Tap in to the feelings this gives you. See if you feel drawn to God in a new way.

Kathy Carlton Willis is God's Grin Gal. She writes and speaks with a balance of funny and faith—whimsy and wisdom. Over a thousand of Kathy's articles have been published, and she has several books in her Grin Gal brand. Kathy graduated with honors from Bible college and has served 30+ years in full-time ministry. Check out her Grin & Grow Break video devotions on social media. www.kathycarltonwillis.com

Grief to Gratitude

Joanie Shawhan

66 **T**his is the place!" **My** best friend and I agreed after numerous apartment walk-throughs. At first, we searched for an apartment for me. Then her living situation changed, and we decided to look for a place together. Apartment hunting had proved challenging. We required certain hard-to-find specifications since she walked with crutches—first floor, a stairless entry, and an elevator for garage access.

She had resigned from her job due to health reasons related to cerebral palsy and looked forward to spending her time praying for people and offering spiritual counseling. Since she couldn't live alone, she needed a living situation that supported her ministry goals. I had experienced healing and restoration under her ministry for over five years and supported her calling. Along with many others, I honored Carol Ann as a friend and mentor.

We laughed and chatted as we headed to the office to sign the rental agreement, excited about our new two-bedroom, two-bathroom apartment. We knew God had chosen this sunny and cheerful home for us.

An unwelcome thought popped into my mind. What if I have to take sole responsibility for her care? I recalled a bout of pneumonia, her most recent brush with death. I shuddered.

Let the Good Times Roll

Carol Ann reflected the love of God more than anyone I had ever known. Our home evolved into a revolving door of ministry as she counseled and prayed for many people. We hosted prayer meetings and Bible studies. Together, we travelled the United States, including Hawaii and Alaska, via planes, cars, and boats to attend Christian conferences.

Multiple surgeries and therapies had robbed her childhood. But God is a God of restoration. He showered her with the things she loved, including a menagerie of stuffed cats—Siamese, lions, tigers, and black panthers. He provided her with a wheelchair, which we pushed through wild cat exhibits at various zoos. She thrilled each time a lion roared.

During her childhood, programs for the disabled had offered pontoon and amphibious rides, which contributed to her love of boats. She coaxed me into joining her water adventures. Her eyes sparkled as we skimmed across the waves in a variety of boats—pontoons, speedboats, riverboats, sailboats, and cruise ships. I prayed my motion sickness medication would stave off the nausea.

Roller coasters, especially water rides, were her theme park favorites. Our friends and I lifted her up onto the front seat of the ride and then cowered behind her as the water splashed our faces and soaked our clothing. She screamed in glee. Her handicap guaranteed us an extra spin or two.

Her child-like faith transformed every activity, every shopping trip into a fun-filled Holy Spirit adventure. Her contagious joy reflected Jesus and transformed the spiritual climate wherever she went.

I Didn't Sign Up for This

Year after year, I witnessed the loss of her independence as her health deteriorated. Her mobility slid from crutch-walking to an electric wheelchair. One day, she struggled for an hour to pull herself up into her wheelchair, but she couldn't muster the strength. Tears pooled in her eyes as she released her grip on the armrests and flopped onto the floor. Her shoulders sagged. She crawled back to her room. She had finally succumbed to immobility. She slept on the floor, propped up with multiple pillows to minimize the pain from severe scoliosis. With all of her necessities within reach, her world, and subsequently my world, narrowed. Our adventures ceased.

I worked twelve-hour nights as a critical care nurse. Squeezed between stress at work and caregiving at home, my treadmill of responsibilities raced faster and faster. Exhaustion and frustration left me feeling hopeless. I snatched a few moments of rest and peace when I ran errands. I'd sit on a bench at a nearby park, hoping to collect my thoughts. My alone time. A respite from the constant demands pulling at the threads of my sanity.

She did her best to make my life less difficult. I did my best to make her comfortable. I felt frustrated that I couldn't help her breathing, impaired by scoliosis, or relieve the constant pain coursing through her back and legs.

I'm a fixer. I'm supposed to make things better, have the right answers to every problem. I expected God to do more, to change her circumstances, to intervene in my way and in my time. But God didn't meet my expectations. Disappointment and helplessness overwhelmed me.

It seemed the more we prayed, the worse her agony. I blamed God. How could a loving God allow one of his children to suffer such excruciating pain and loss of function?

I felt spiritually dry, weary, and angry. I was afraid. Afraid I would lose my best friend. Even though I faithfully read the Scriptures and prayed, I choked on the words. The little faith I mustered quickly drained away. Nothing I did seemed to relieve her suffering. My heart broke.

The Voice of Truth

One night, while she snagged a little sleep between bouts of pain, I stole into the living room and slipped into my rocker. I opened my Bible and prayed. God felt distant and far away. My prayers didn't seem to reach the ceiling, let alone the throne room of heaven. I railed at him and accused him of not listening or caring. *Where are you, God?*

A word flashed across my mind. *Gratitude*. I needed to be grateful. Grateful for what? For day-in and day-out stress, pain, and exhaustion?

I had no clue where to begin. I glanced around the room and grappled with the words as I thanked God for a roof over my head, my car, my job, my friends, and my eyes to see. Thanking God for legs to walk plumbed the depths of my ungrateful heart, especially since Carol Ann could no longer walk, even with crutches. My ingratitude appalled me.

The voices of bitterness, resentment, and fear had clamored for my attention for so long, they blocked the whispers of God and blinded me to his goodness. I failed to recognize how my destructive thoughts spilled from my lips in the form of grumbling and complaining. I asked God to forgive me for my ingratitude and blaming him for our suffering.

I lingered in the Psalms. David had poured out his heart to God in his suffering. But he also worshipped. In his worship he experienced the presence of God. And joy. David's example of a life filled with thanksgiving and praise provided me with a roadmap through suffering and into the presence of God. A presence that brings fullness of joy. Thankfulness unlocked my heart.

Carol Ann understood these truths, even in the midst of her pain. Sometimes tears streamed down her cheeks as she declared God's truth through gritted teeth. "Our God is in the heavens, and he does as he wishes" (Psalm 115:3).

I never understood why God allowed her to suffer. But he reminded me that his thoughts are higher than my thoughts, and his ways are far beyond anything I could imagine.

The Lord's response trumped mine. I needed to let go of my control and admit he is God, and I am not.

Not My Will But Yours

I wish I could say our circumstances changed, but they didn't. Carol Ann gradually succumbed to complications from cerebral palsy. She taught me the Scriptures and prayed a deposit of prayers for me from which I could draw after she passed. I am who I am today because of her investment in me.

God's peace and comfort melted the remnants of anger in my heart. Would the anger have dissipated if I had not embarked on a journey of gratitude? I don't know. But I would rather go through difficult circumstances with God's presence than rage at him for not doing things my way and so miss his comfort and peace.

I had allowed ingratitude to obscure his goodness and almost missed the gift he had given me in Carol Ann. Her child-like faith bubbled with a contagious joy that spilled over all who were around her. A joy that overshadowed her handicap and pain. A joy I would have missed had I remained stuck in a thankless heart attitude. Even in the middle of my heartache, I experienced the presence of God.

Today, when I question God and wrestle with unanswered prayer, I remember that night, alone in my living room—angry, dejected, and empty. I thank God for his faithfulness. His loving hand guided me into a course correction—a journey to gratitude.

Renew and Restore

- Think about a time you felt discouraged due to difficult circumstances. Consider making a list of blessings and answered prayers. Remember God's goodness and give thanks.
- If you have been a caregiver for a family member or dear friend, where have you seen God show up in the midst of the hard times?
- Where have you found hope and encouragement in God's Word in difficult times? Write a note with a verse to send to a friend.

Joanie Shawhan is a Selah Awards Finalist for *In Her Shoes: Dancing in the Shadow of Cancer.* She is an ovarian cancer survivor, registered nurse, speaker, and media guest. She speaks to medical students in the Survivors Teaching Students program and co-founded an ovarian cancer social group, The Fried Eggs—Sunny-Side Up. When not attending her book clubs or writing critique group, Joanie enjoys swimming, knitting, and playing the autoharp.

Finding the Road to Belief

Michele Morin

The *buzz of cafeteria noise* receded to the background as I bowed my head to thank God for the contents of my plastic tray. Hitting PLAY on the mental tape labeled "blessing the food," I was alarmed when the tired, empty words snagged and snarled inside my head.

"Where are you, God?" I asked the roaring emptiness. "Are you even here?"

An Unexpected Unraveling

My faith unraveled at a Christian college. I know that isn't the way it's supposed to happen. I can remember wishing that a hostile, atheistic professor had bludgeoned me into my doubts with brilliantly irrefutable arguments. It would make for a much better story.

Instead, the truth is I just got numb. Somehow, faith in Christ had been reduced to a constant barrage of meaningless requirements that were mysteriously related to Christianity. Plowing through a three-inch thick commentary on Romans with no specific assignment in mind (other than to reach the back cover). Fending off the desperate and over-bearing overtures of my dorm mother, who wanted to befriend all "her girls." Trying to stay awake while the combed-over, suited-up preacher-of-the-day got carried away and stole time from the class that followed our mandatory chapel. One day, it all got to be just too ridiculous.

Eventually, of course, I realized that the problem was localized and that what I had been objecting to was not "Christianity" itself but a mind-set that existed on a particular campus, in a specific zip code, during a season long past. Having said that, it would seem that the road back to faith would have been like flipping a switch—yesterday I doubted, but today I am choosing to believe. However, calluses on the soul are even tougher than the ones on the soles of our feet, and it's a long exfoliation that thins their numbing presence.

The Road Back to Believing

My first mistake in trying to live my way back into faith was looking in the wrong direction. There is no going back into a former faith. There is only going forward. In looking for yesterday's faith experience, I was forgetting that I was not the same kind of believer as I had been before. Even so, mysteriously and graciously, through the blur of career and ministry, then marriage and four children, a sprout of faith was growing again, but in a brand-new way. This time, I was guided by truth rather than by the "experts," attempting to live in the moment of showing a spring daffodil to a tiny boy and then sitting on the damp grass to talk about the God who made it.

Always in the back of my mind during this quiet rebirth was the idea that I wanted to do something meaningful for God. Something meaningful, I thought, could only happen if I had to learn another language, live in another culture (the more remote and risky, the better), or, most importantly, if I could see results for my efforts.

Unfortunately, this was the polar opposite of what I happened to be doing at the time, which was caring for my young children, trying to write, and shoveling a path through the house every few days. Worshiping at the altar of results, I certainly could not see how ministry (as I defined it) would ever be part of my life again.

Then one day, a back injury flared up, and I was lying on the floor trying to get relief from the daily pain while at the same time entertaining my toddler and baby. Surrounded by building blocks and picture books, I grabbed my Bible for a quick read and was handed a job description from an Old Testament prophet:

> No, O people, the Lord has told you what is good,
>
>> and this is what he requires of you:
>
> to do what is right, to love mercy,
>
>> and to walk humbly with your God. (Micah 6:8)

Something Meaningful for God

There it was, and it made perfect sense. There's nothing like a diaper pail in the bathroom for eleven years to serve as a reminder not to take oneself too seriously. But even after it was retired, there were little boys who mirrored back my character flaws and stretched me to the limits of where I could confidently practice "what is right."

Now, there are four young men who love me well despite all my flaws, and my patient husband of many years shows me every day what compassion and loyalty look like, but most especially on the day when, standing in front of an empty sock drawer, he declared, "Hon, even with all the studying you've been doing lately, you've hardly missed a beat around here." (Is he a keeper, or what?)

For me, finding the way forward doesn't mean that I never look back, but I'm careful how much time I spend looking in the rear-view mirror—either wistfully or regretfully. The doing and the being of my Micah 6:8 job description are all present tense.

Faith Going Forward

It will always be important to me to be learning about God and to be able to articulate what I am learning in some way. But the difference, going forward, is that I really want to stand beside someone else and share the view.

I want to crack open the Word of God and dig for truth as if my life depends on it, to stand in awe of truth that feeds my faith, and then to sit at the table with my Sunday school class and be amazed together. I want to read, and re-read, and read again the words about Jesus that translate ordinary faithfulness into radical discipleship and that transform baked macaroni and cheese and a bowl of home-canned green beans into bread and wine. To put flesh on the bones of God's commandments before my family and my friends, even though I understand that they will see me contradict daily the truth I teach. To read a book that presents theology like a laser show of worship and then pass it along to a friend. To come to the end of a blog post knowing that I understand some aspect of the walk of faith better than I did before I wrote it. To desire God, not as a means to the end of fulfilling my own wishes but as the end himself.

This, for me, is the way forward, and I invite you to stand here beside me and to re-evaluate your own life, to resist anything that has become hollow and formulaic, and to make room for today's faith. Spiritual practices that brought you joy five or ten years ago may need to be tweaked or abandoned altogether as God beckons you further up and further in, deeper into his boundless love.

Unchanged and unchanging, God will meet you today with fresh mercy. He will speak into your lonely silence, for he is here with you, beckoning you into your own way forward.

Renew and Restore

- What is your orientation toward time? Do you find yourself derailed by longing for the past, or are you more likely to gaze into the future to avoid dealing with the pressing issues of the present moment?
- Think back to a season of wandering or unbelief in your own life. What was your process of finding your way forward once again? What stimulated the journey?
- If you are presently experiencing doubts or disdain, can you put your finger on the catalyst that sent you off the rails? If you have a sense that this is a temporary detour, what needs to happen for you to move into a fresh and confident faith?

- Looking at your own faith journey and projecting yourself into a vibrant future faith, what components do you see as being absolutely necessary for your spiritual growth and maturity? What steps can you take today to make this a reality? Write a courageous prayer asking God to give you the ability to move forward with him in fresh faith every day.

Michele Morin is a reader, writer, speaker, and gardener who does life with her family on a country hill in Maine. She has been married to an unreasonably patient husband for thirty years, and together they have four sons, two daughters-in-love, and three adorable grandchildren. Active in educational ministries with her local church, Michele delights in sitting at a table surrounded by women with open Bibles.

Redefined to Thrive

Dr. Marlene Carson

W*ho would have ever thought* that being the paid entertainment at our family functions when I was just eight years old would make me comfortable enough to dance on poles later? I still remember my parents partying, waking up the kids, and giving us quarters to dance for them. When I look back now, I find it interesting that I was the only one who received dollars to dance. At the time, I didn't understand why I was told not to tell momma that I got twenty dollars just for sitting on my uncle's lap. Now, I realize that I was passed around at an early age—to cousins, uncles, and family friends.

Pieces of me were scattered everywhere, while I was left broken and ashamed. This is the environment that I came out of, but that is not where I came from.

The light of truth shines on the pathway of liberation, dispelling all manner of darkness, removing the cataracts from our mind's eye so that we may clearly see that we will never again walk through life tripping and stumbling like a drunk who has lost control of their senses—having no direction at all.

For me, the light of truth shined through Jeremiah 29:11, "'For I know the plans I have for you,' says the LORD. 'They are plans for good and not for disaster, to give you a future and a hope.'" That Scripture would continually prove its truth in my life through my environment, situations, and even my relationships.

My story—past, present, and future—was simultaneously known in the mind of God even before the start of my lineage. Established in the mind of God—the many transitions, private victories, and public deliverances all a part of a process, a process that doesn't lead me to a happy conclusion, but "an expected end," as one translation of that Scripture says. In this Scripture, God showed how he had a future and a hope for the shattered nation of Israel, and he surely had one for me too.

With that in mind, my past—once filled with shadows of intimidation and insecurity—has become my testimony. A shadow doesn't exist unless light shines upon its subject—the light of God's truth. Truth that shines within the world of adult entertainment. Truth that shines in abusive relationships. Truth that even shines in the Christian church, shining to dispel the darkness.

Jesus said, "And you will know the truth, and the truth will set you free'" (John 8:32). I have known the intimacy of truth, setting me free from strip clubs, escort services, and pimps who hang in the darkest of motels, as well as those who stand behind the most ornate pulpits. This truth has made me free:

> The Spirit of the Sovereign Lord is upon me,
>> for the Lord has anointed me
>> to bring good news to the poor.
> He has sent me to comfort the brokenhearted
>> and to proclaim that captives will be released
>> and prisoners will be freed. (Isaiah 61:1)

This truth is only found in the Word of God, through the love of God, and being in relationship with God. For me, that truth had to be discovered.

Resentful

You may not have experienced sex trafficking, but sexual abuse comes with very similar trauma. Like a peeping Tom watching me from afar, my trafficker began to capture my intrinsic nature and the indispensable quality of who I was without ever having a conversation with me. Studying me, not for the purpose of supplying my every need but to use it against me when I didn't obey his every command. By the time I actually heard his voice, the game had already begun, and I didn't even know the rules, the players, or even how to play the game. Like the disease of high blood pressure, because of my smile, my situation went undetected to my friends and family.

He knew what he was doing—the trafficker, that is—when he began to keep me away from my family and friends, isolating me from my normal life and causing me to depend solely on him.

It was all a part of his plan for my life that turned me so bitter and cold. I'm talking about the kind of cold that soaks through your soul. No thermometer and no thermostat could ever measure that dire extreme. For me, cold had nothing to do with the degrees on a thermostat or the temperature outside. The chill that crept into my character caused me to isolate, leaving me craving to be properly touched while robbing me of the ability to feel. I didn't understand why this had to happen to me. I was not the promiscuous girl, the drug-addicted girl, or even the prettiest girl. What he saw in me had nothing to do with looks, sex, or addiction. It had everything to do with power and control that he could exercise over my weakness and vulnerability.

The trafficker created the illusion of a better life, a beautifully functioning family, and exceeding my daily needs. That was all he had to do to keep me engaged. I soon discovered my reality was cloaked in a mystery that was just as cold as Minnesota in the wintertime. I was being trafficked.

Redeemed

Life after exploitation was very hard. Most people I spoke with, trained, or even went to church with thought I should just shake it off and just be grateful that I was safely home with my family. I couldn't do that, though. I was bitter, broken, and angry—even angry at God. I ask you not to judge me for being honest.

Have you ever been mad at God? You see, I just didn't understand, *Why me?* Why couldn't I be the girl that went from high school to college, chose a nice career path, married the man of my dreams, bought a house with a white picket fence, and had two kids and a dog? After all, that was the American dream, right?

By this time in my life, my innocence, along with my dreams, had been stolen. The idea of an authentic relationship was an utter fantasy until one day when I went to church. The pastor was preaching a message from the book of Hosea. He titled it "Don't You Know That You've Been Purchased." The pastor was killing me softly with his words. I remembered sitting on the edge of the pew listening to my life story being told to the congregation. At least it felt as if he was talking about me. Has that ever happened to you? You went to church, and it seemed like the pastor was talking directly to you *about you?*

A woman named Gomer was sold on an auction block then purchased by Hosea. God told this prophet to marry a prostitute—to love her and cherish her as his wife. *What?* Today people would say, "God wouldn't do that." He wouldn't tell a godly man to marry a prostitute! I am here to tell you, God *did* that! He used that example in the Bible to show how much he loves us, past and all.

I found so much love, healing, and restoration in that story that I began to live it out. I know that my soul has been redeemed by the sacrifice of Jesus, who paid the ransom with his blood. I, too, have been bought with a price and have his secure promise that I am his child. I couldn't be happier! Even in the most difficult times, the joy I have found in Christ has become my strength.

The journey to wholeness has not always been easy. It has been a long and winding road, but it is a journey that not only leads you to a happy conclusion but also a future and a hope.

Renew and Restore

- What situations or experiences have caused you to redefine your life?
- When have you been mad at God for circumstances that didn't go the way you had hoped? If you haven't already told him, write it out in your journal or tell him in prayer. He can handle your honesty.
- God wants to remove shame and restore your heart. That begins with having a relationship with him first. The next step is getting to know him and what it means to be his child. The book of Ephesians (in the New Testament) is a great place to begin learning about what it means to be part of God's family.

Dr. Marlene Carson, SurThrivalist, survivor of domestic minor sex trafficking, member of the U.S. Advisory Council on Trafficking, minister, author, and inventor of the Peerpreneur Movement, is one of America's foremost authorities on sex trafficking. Many may have a textbook knowledge of the perils of exploitation, but Marlene knows from her own personal experience. At age fifteen, she became one of the tens of thousands of girls and young adult women who are exploited daily. www.marlenecarson.com

To Forgive Is to Be Free

Alba Corva

Even as a young child, I knew I was different from the rest of my family. A child should never be seen as a freak or unworthy of being part of the family, but I was. I was interested in literature, art, and the human mind. My family scoffed at my interests and treated me as if I was foolish for liking these things. My personality was beyond their understanding or acceptance, and they did not forgive me for it. Although we were different, I still felt as if I was a part of them, that I belonged. That belief changed very abruptly one night.

I was around seven years old, and I went into my mother's room in tears because some of the other children in school were teasing me, saying that I was a freak. After I told her what happened, I begged her for advice, hoping and praying in my childish mind that my mommy could make things better.

She waited a moment, as if contemplating her words. I thought the silence would kill me with each passing second. When she did speak, she said only one sentence, but a sentence that still breaks my heart so many years later.

"Maybe tomorrow you should try to be normal."

It's amazing how eight simple words can change a person. After I left her room that night, I crawled into bed, but I did not sleep. I laid awake for what felt like hours, not believing what I had heard. I tried to come up with other meanings behind her words, but there was no point because I knew the truth.

My mother agreed with my bullies. She thought I was a freak too.

As the rest of the house slept, I stared up at the ceiling and silently thought out a prayer. I prayed that I would wake up and forget what happened. I prayed that everything would be alright in school the next day with the other kids who had picked on me. But most of all, I prayed for strength because I knew that my previous prayers were not going to come true. I would never be able to forget, and everything was not going to be alright in school.

A Life Unwanted

After that night, I began to pay more attention to what my family said to me. I paid attention when my mother would refer to me as her accident, her happy accident. I paid attention when my family would joke about how I should have been born into a different family. And I paid attention when my family would tell me to shut up because they said that they did not care about what I had to say.

I stayed in solitude and silence most of the time when I was at home because they had made it perfectly clear that my voice was not welcome. I made it through because I knew that someone *did* love me. Every Sunday, we would go to church, and I would listen with joy, knowing that I had a heavenly parent who genuinely cared about me. I made it through because every night, I would speak to that loving parent, and I would always ask for the same thing in every prayer. "Please give me strength."

Strength in an Unexpected Place

Every night I prayed for strength, but it took many years to finally see the strength I had already been given. I'd felt so alone in the world. But the moment when I found the strength I had prayed about for so long was a moment that most people would never suspect.

I had been writing for many years by that time, but I had never really shown my work to anyone. I didn't feel as if I could trust anybody with what I had worked so hard on. I wrote a novel and self-published it with fear in my heart because I didn't know what to expect. Even though I was afraid, I am so happy that I went through with it.

The moment when everything changed for me, and I finally saw my strength, was when I held my first book in my hands. Within those pages, I had released my pain with every word. Although it was fictional, the characters became the closest friends I have ever had. Writing their story gave me the support I needed to make it through each day. If I felt any pain, I knew that they would be there. I just needed to start writing.

I left my old home in Kentucky not too long after that and made a new home in Florida. With my newfound strength, I reinvented myself. I was no longer the accident child that I was always told that I was. I was now a strong woman who could finally stand on her own two feet, with the help of a loving Father.

With the guiding hand of that loving Father, I accomplished things that my family never expected me to do. As of this moment, I have written ten books, I have a master's degree in clinical mental health, I have a well-paying job, and I am buying my own house—all at age twenty-four. Even though I have accomplished so many things in my life, I'll never forget the loving Parent who brought me to where I am today. I never forget because when I go to bed and say my prayers, I always ask the same thing. "Please give me strength."

Finding Forgiveness in a Broken Heart

Although my family took me to church, they never showed me what the teachings of kindness and love truly meant. My family did provide for me in the ways of food and shelter, but they did not provide me what I really needed—love and acceptance. To anyone who reads this, be they a friend or stranger, know that I pray you will find love and acceptance. I lived so long without it, so I know the value of those pure joys. I found love and acceptance when I decided to forgive, to finally let go.

That moment of forgiveness came to me within a dark moment. Death is something that passes through our minds at least every once in a while. At that time, those thoughts invaded more and more frequently. I had moments like this before that I had never told anybody about, but this one was worse than the others. I was in the shower, my tears disappearing among the water from the falling stream. I cried, thinking about all the pressures I was feeling, how I was being treated in school, and how my family had once again made fun of me without anyone coming to my defense. It is a truly isolating feeling to believe that you are your only ally.

As I felt my tears beginning to fade, I watched the water swirl down the drain as if hypnotized by it. In my distressed mind, a strange thought came to me. *Water is seen as a precious thing to so many people, yet I am wasting it.* A second thought came over me just as quickly. *Are you going to waste something as precious as your life like you are wasting the water?*

I turned the water off almost immediately. A third thought rushed through my mind, a thought that has influenced me to this day. *Are you really everything your family and the people around you have always said that you are?* Whenever I had looked in the mirror, I saw the accident, the freak, the unwanted child.

As I got out of the shower and looked in the mirror, though, that image was gone. Instead, I saw a young woman with pain hidden behind innocent eyes. The priests in every church I have been to have always stated that God loves every one of us for who we are. He created us, so none of us is a mistake. If that was true, then how could I be a mistake? At that moment, I found myself letting go of every word the people around me ever said. At that moment, I forgave them.

I had buried anger in my heart with every negative action they committed against me, and it was only when I let that go and gave myself permission to forgive them that the anger finally began to disappear. I never stated my forgiveness to them personally because they never acknowledged they had wronged me. The forgiveness was only within my own heart and soul, but that was all I needed.

What my family did to me as a child still hurts me in my heart, but I have forgiven them. I have always loved them. Please do not think otherwise. I could never hate my family. My only wish was that things could have been different. My parents have been kinder to me as of recently, although we still don't really talk that much. Some things never change. They do have the capacity for love and acceptance. I have seen them readily give that to my siblings, but I was never accepted, and I don't believe I ever will be.

What they did wasn't right, but my loving Father always taught me that you should forgive those who wrong you. If you don't, hatred will form in your soul. I have already spent so many years with pain and hatred inside me, I don't want to waste any more time thinking about the past. I want to focus on today and tomorrow.

I may have only a few yesterdays, and I cannot do anything about them, but I have countless tomorrows ahead, and I want to enjoy every single one with love, acceptance, and forgiveness in my heart. The darkness tries to appear every once in a while, but I don't give it permission to take over. It tries to invade sometimes, and the hatred returns, but when I recognize it, I find space alone so that I can talk with the only One who has always loved and accepted me—my heavenly Father. When I do that, the darkness flees from my heart.

Renew and Restore

- When have you felt as if you didn't belong? How did you respond?
- Your accomplishments aren't what defines your value. Describe what God sees in you that has nothing to do with achievements or performance.
- Sometimes the person who hurt us will never acknowledge it. Explain how we can still forgive, even if they never ask.

Alba Corva is a therapist who works to try and rid others of their darkness. She has been writing for many years and has authored books mainly for young adults and children. These books are designed to examine the darkness within and around us and combat it. Miss Corva lives with her cat in her home in Florida. She is a devout Catholic who hopes to one day inspire others to find inspiration within her writing.

My Coming of (Middle) Age

Darla Grieco

Stepping off the bus, *I* inhaled the woodsy scent of the Western Pennsylvania mountains, the breeze rustling the leaves above. A still lake at the base of the camp caught my attention. I imagined myself sipping coffee by the water's edge at sunrise with the mist hovering just above the surface. Suddenly, a fellow traveler caught the back of my knees with his luggage. Stumbling, I snarled in his direction.

"Sorry," the boy said in snarky, elementary-aged fashion. I sighed, quietly admonishing myself for thinking I would actually be able to relax while here. I knew better, especially since this trip was about my daughter, not me.

The time had come for our daughter, Katelyn, to attend her Rite of Passage fifth grade field trip—a three-day, two-night excursion to a YMCA camp called Deer Valley. The district planned the event each spring to give the students from all three elementary schools an opportunity to meet other children in preparation to enter the middle school the following fall. I hoped and prayed that *my daughter* would embrace this time away, to grow and make new friends. Little did I know, God had plans for me as well.

"Parents," our fearless leader pulled me back to task, "your cabin and kid assignments are in your folders. Drop off your luggage and be in the mess hall in fifteen minutes."

I consulted the rosters in my folder, where I found three separate lists—dining mates, bunkmates, and team-building mates—all names I didn't recognize. Except for my daughter. I knew her and only her.

I rarely spent any time away from my little family—one husband, my Katelyn, and her three siblings, also in elementary school. I loved them, and they consumed me. I'd spent the prior twelve years serving them as wife and mother. I folded laundry, made meals, did the shopping—a far cry from what I imagined myself doing when the dean of education handed me my master's degree or when the human resource gal handed me my first employment contract. Though I didn't mind leaving all that behind me to raise my family, somewhere in those years of service, I lost track of who I was. My dreams. My purpose.

Oh, right. My purpose now was to keep the children in my care safe, disciplined, and alive, and I was determined to make the best of it. This trip would be no different. Straightening my spine to its full, upright position, I flashed my daughter a reassuring smile. "Well, let's find our cabin."

The Adventure Begins

We made our way to the small metal building where we would sleep the next two nights. With most of the beds already claimed, we put our stuff on the remaining bunks and headed for the mess hall.

Two other parents and six children welcomed us to our table. As we greeted one another, an old familiar heat rose up my chest, flushing my cheeks. My heart raced. I couldn't believe how this simple task forced me far from my comfort zone. Idle chit chat? I'd lost my touch.

After lunch, we found the group of parents and students we would be spending the most time with during our trip. Team-building activities awaited us throughout the camp, requiring the students to work together in an attempt to create camaraderie among them.

As for camaraderie among the adults, the task with this group proved much easier. One of the mothers who I did recall meeting before had a vibrant personality. *I'll cling to her*, I thought. As I suspected, she took to the task of introducing all the parents to one another. I smiled nicely at each until one woman, in particular, struck me as very familiar.

"This is Beth," Vicki said.

I knew I'd seen her somewhere before. "Have we met?"

She agreed I looked familiar, but neither of us could place where we had crossed paths. We reviewed the places we frequented: the bank, her place of employment, kids' activities.

Nothing.

We continued to fulfill our chaperone duties, including a hike up Mt. Davis, shooting bows and arrows, and learning about plants and birds of the region. As adults, our job was to observe and encourage the children in their assigned tasks but never to intervene. I struggled to keep my parental opinion to myself but obeyed the rules. The time had come for me to let go of my controlling mommy ways and, instead, enjoy the little things such as the crunching of the pine needles on the forest floor. I tried to relax.

New Games

Late on our first day, we arrived at a station called New Games, hosted by a fourth-grade teacher, Dr. Brecht, whom I had never met before. She called all the members of both teams to line up at the edge of a field.

Parents, too?

Not I, I thought.

I beelined for the wooden benches off to the edge of the field and took up my best ladylike position. Legs crossed, hands resting on my knees.

"Excuse me. You, over there," Dr. Brecht's sing-songy voice called out from the field.

I put a finger to my chest and gave the teacher my best perplexed expression.

"C'mon," she prodded. "You can't just sit there. Let's have some fun!"

Fun? I thought. She couldn't be serious. I'm a mother. We sit on the sidelines for dance recitals, soccer practices, and the like. We don't *play*.

I quickly realized I was fighting a losing battle. Not wanting to make a scene, I reluctantly agreed to join the others.

"Now, everyone," she said. "Untie one shoe. Right. Left. I don't care, but I want to see who can fling their shoe the farthest into this field. But there is a catch. If you hit me, you buy me a new pair of shoes."

I stood with my mouth agape. *Hit you?* She stood hundreds of feet away in the middle of a field. I looked at the ten-year-olds on either side of me. *Is this woman insane?* And then, it occurred to me, if I did what she commanded, I'd be standing here with only one shoe. Hives began to creep up my chest yet again. I looked longingly toward my bench—that place of safety and security. But it was too late.

The first flinger had already removed his shoe, and we all watched as it sailed through the air toward Dr. Brecht. Then, the second child went, and a third. Shoes were flying off feet one after the next. The children laughed and cheered one another on. Their energy and excitement invigorated my spirit. I fought tears that threatened to spill forth as a new emotion I hadn't felt in a long time began to surface. *What is this feeling?* For twelve tiring years, I was the grown-up. Day in and day out, I acted grown up and had forgotten how to play.

I can do this, I thought. *I will do this!*

And then the time had come. With one sneaker dangling on the edge of my toes, I clunked back a few steps. I leaned in like a runner awaiting a gunshot and raced to the kicking line. I swung my leg with all my might and watched as my shoe soared up and outward, spinning through the air. Joy welled up inside of me.

That felt amazing! I watched and waited as my shoe hit the ground, bounced, and tumbled just beyond the record kick.

"We have a new winner!" Dr. Brecht shouted. "Come on out here and stand by your shoe."

Suddenly, I found myself playing and having genuine, silly fun.

As I stood out there alone in the field, Dr. Brecht huddled with my competitors to make a plan to overthrow my success. The parents and children began to playfully taunt me from the sidelines.

"We're taking you down, Mrs. Grieco!"

"You don't stand a chance!"

I puffed out my chest and sensed my body had been overtaken by the same spirit as when Dr. Bruce Banner turned into the Incredible Hulk. I hunkered down and flexed my muscles.

"Bring it on," I shouted.

Dr. Brecht drew back as if she, too, were shocked at my transformation.

For the next ten minutes, everyone laughed and cheered as the group tried to beat my record. As for me, I felt freer than I had in years.

Little did I know, God was not done with me yet.

You Matter To Me

Shortly after that, the parents from my team and I stood by the trickling stream as the children searched for salamanders. Beth and I still hadn't figured out where we'd met until, suddenly, she turned to me and pointed a finger in my direction. "Isaiah 54:5," she said.

"Excuse me?"

"You gave me that Scripture. 'For your Maker is your husband—the LORD Almighty is his name . . .'" (NIV).

I stood there, blinking at her. Waiting.

"I came to Bible studies at your house," she motioned toward our daughters, who were now heading off to sixth grade, "when these two were babies."

I fought tears for the second time that day as Beth continued to tell me how the Scripture I gave her many years prior had carried her through a difficult time in her life. "I treasure it to this day," she said.

It occurred to me that almost a decade had passed since she came to my home, but something I said touched her life. She appreciated it. She appreciated me. I realized that while the things we do can change in different seasons of our lives, God can still bless what we do.

That day, God reminded me that I didn't need a corporate job or to speak before masses of people as a successful psychologist to affect someone. I could be of service right where I was, even if it only helped one person at a time. Just like I made a difference in Beth's life so many years ago, Dr. Brecht helped me by pulling me out of my shell and making me realize I could still have fun.

Two Butterflies Emerged

While we sat around the campfire on our final evening, Dr. Brecht awarded me as the Shoe Fling Champion of our group. I accepted my certificate, knowing I was taking away much more. Like a butterfly waking from a cocoon, I learned to laugh and play again.

My daughter and I both left Deer Valley changed. She met some new friends and felt more confident to enter the next season of her life at the middle school. And I, too, felt more confident to enter the next season of my life doing whatever God had in store.

Renew and Restore

- Can you recall clearly defined seasons in your life—employee, student, caretaker, parent, etc.? Make a list of your seasons and record one valuable lesson you learned from each.
- Laughter is good for the spirit. What are some healthy ways you could have fun and play? Schedule time to complete at least one of these activities each week for one month.

Darla Grieco has published in Guideposts *Angels on Earth* magazine and in various Chicken Soup for the Soul editions. In the spring of 2021, several of her devotions appeared in a compilation titled *Wit, Whimsy & Wisdom*. You can read more from Darla at dsgrieco.com.

Surrendered Heart's Desire

Diana Leagh Matthews

As a little girl, I remember having the story read to me about the old woman in the shoe who had so many children she didn't know what to do. Even at that young age, I knew all I wanted to be was a wife and mother. During those early years, I lined all my baby dolls and stuffed animals up for tea parties and to play house.

As an only child, I began to ask for a baby sister or brother from a young age. I had to wait nine and eleven years for those blessings, but once they arrived, they were my "babies." I enjoyed loving and doting on them and being Mama's helper. Even our dog, Lacey, did not escape my desire for motherhood. From the time she was a puppy, I would wrap her up in a towel and sit with her in our family rocker.

A Dream for the Future

By the time I became a teenager, I fell asleep dreaming about when I would be married and have children of my own. I wanted at least two sons and two daughters and even had names picked out. I dreamed of the toddlers who would one day run around. Then, as teenagers they would have friends who would join us and drop in for a slice of pizza, to dance to music, to discuss their problems, or even for a slumber party.

When I married at eighteen, I thought all my dreams were about to come true. But the union proved to be short-lived and childless. My heart broke with the lost dreams and the struggles ahead. Resentment began to take root in my mind and heart.

Ten years after my marriage ended, another relationship came along. From the beginning, I made it clear how important children were and listened to all the promises made. Little did I know how empty those promises were and the tumultuous life I would have in that three-year abusive relationship.

By the time I left that relationship, my heart and spirit were broken. I returned to my parents' home, wondering if my dreams would ever come true. Two months after returning home, my sister gave birth to her second son. While I was happy for her, envy also welled within me. What was wrong with me? Why couldn't I have the one thing I always wanted and dreamed of?

I spent many nights crying out to God, asking for answers—which didn't seem to come—and begging not to be resentful for my sister's happiness.

A Dream Unfulfilled

Part of the healing journey meant digging deep and dealing with the loss of my dreams. As I turned forty, I struggled with the realization I would never become a mother. For three years, a battle waged within me as I tried to come to terms with reality and the loss of this dream. Eventually, I accepted the fact that I would never be a mother—at least not in the traditional way.

A friend told me of someone she knew who adopted three brothers to give them a home, and another acquaintance took in teen sisters. Couldn't I follow in their footsteps? But sadly, my financial situation didn't allow me this possibility.

There are still days when I curl up on the couch and cry as the loneliness overwhelms me, but I've learned that it helps to remind myself of all the ways in which I am blessed.

A Different Kind of Family

For over five years, I have worked in a nursing home as an activities director. Over this time, I have incorporated the feeling of a family with the residents. The needs are plentiful, and when I am buried in paperwork and don't have time with them, I discover how much I miss the residents. I've come to love them, and they show they love me too. They have a safe place to come and express their heart, concerns, and desires with my staff and me.

For the past few years, we have gathered around our large table for a "family" Thanksgiving dinner. Serving over twenty residents at one large table is not for the faint of heart. It becomes systematic as we hand out the silverware and drinks and prepare everyone's plates. We even created a system for posting the menu and marking what each person didn't want. This allows the process of serving to run smoother.

While serving them their Thanksgiving dinner recently, one lady looked at me and said, "You're like the old lady who lived in the shoe. She had so many children she didn't know what to do." The statement made me pause and think a moment. Then I laughed. She had a point. My heart felt light and happy.

"You're right."

I looked around the table at the faces of all my precious "children," each with their own personalities, needs, abilities, and interests. Somehow, as unlikely as it seemed, we had become a family.

Unanswered Prayers

Later, while home and able to rest, the Lord spoke to me. "I've been providing children for you all along. You just didn't see it."

I thought back over the years and the variety of "children" the Lord had provided. From working with kids, teens, and seniors in the church setting to teaching all ages through private music lessons. Then there are over twenty years of caregiving in a variety of capacities, as well as mentoring the teenage interns and volunteers at the nursing home. Yes, the Lord had provided—just not in the way I expected.

Turning to Scripture, I stumbled upon the verse that speaks of the barren woman having more children than the woman with children.

"'Sing, O childless woman, you who have never given birth! Break into loud and joyful song, O Jerusalem, you who have never been in labor. For the desolate woman now has more children than the woman who lives with her husband,' says the LORD" (Isaiah 54:1). Yes, God had provided and given me children—even when it wasn't what I planned or the way I wanted.

Although the passage uses the barren woman as a metaphor for Jerusalem and the Israelites in captivity, it provided comfort and hope for me that God has a plan and is in control. Even when I don't understand.

Just because God doesn't answer prayers in the way we would hope doesn't mean he doesn't care. There have been times I've had to work on my heart and attitude as I've become jaded, discouraged, and downtrodden by the lack of answers. That's when I need to raise my eyes upward and praise the Lord—even when I don't understand or like the answers. At times it's a struggle and a process, but I choose to keep my eyes and heart focused heavenward.

The Greatest Gift

I'm learning that some of life's greatest gifts are unanswered prayers.

When we held our Christmas party at the senior living home, my heart sang with happiness as I handed each resident their stack of Christmas presents. This is what it's like to have a huge family Christmas celebration together. My heart burst with joy, and I couldn't think of a sweeter feeling or moment. These precious "children" make me feel loved, wanted, needed, and appreciated in countless ways.

While I'll never know the reason my childhood dreams were not fulfilled, the Lord has met my needs and provided in other ways. And I trust that when my days in healthcare come to a close and God leads me down other paths, the doors will open to serve others, love them, and have a sense of family—only it'll look different from what others have. But the Lord's been teaching me that families come in all sizes, shapes, and gatherings.

Renew and Restore

- What unanswered dream do you have? How does your life look different than what you envisioned?
- How has God met your needs in other ways in your life?
- How can you show God's love to others in unconventional and unexpected ways? See if you can identify one person or group of people who could use encouragement and connection.
- Write out a prayer to God, thanking him for both answered prayers and disappointments. Tell him what's on your heart and ask him to show you blessings you hadn't noticed before.

Diana Leagh Matthews has numerous stories to share, often from her job as an activities director, where she wears many hats, including Bible teacher, vocalist, historian, and event planner. She has four prayer books scheduled for publication in 2021 but is a novelist at heart. Check out her hymn stories and Bible studies at www.DianaLeaghMatthews.com and her hymn-votions on social media.

Where Faith and Suffering Collide

Terri Prahl

Have you ever lived your life in a way that was inconsistent with what you proclaimed to believe? Ever experienced a moment when reality instantaneously collided with the faith you held, leading you to doubt and question everything you regarded as true?

At the age of twenty-four, I experienced pregnancy and the wonder of motherhood for the first time. With great affection, we named him Ryan Todd, and I carried him in my belly with pride and joy. My husband and I excitedly made plans for fitting our son into a tiny, one-bedroom, cinderblock wall apartment once he outgrew my body and made his grand entrance. From the beginning, I busied myself with mothering this little guy who constantly squirmed and kicked against my ribs. I never imagined anything outside of God granting us a healthy baby boy.

The day after delivery, a nurse wheeled me through the hospital to where my husband waited to help me into the car. As she pushed me through the halls, I fidgeted with the dangling hospital bracelets irritating my wrist, avoided the pitying glances from staff, and slumped in the unease of my empty arms and broken heart.

Our son, Ryan, had been stillborn.

In that wheelchair moment, my theology about who I was to God and what he promised to me was challenged. Nothing made sense. Deep down, I had always believed God would protect and answer my prayers of earnest faith. I had been taught to believe without wavering and that according to John 14:13, anything I asked in his name would be granted to me. My prayerful expectation had been for protection, health, and a life full of joy. When my reality clashed with my understanding of God, I began a journey of reordering my affections and asking God to give me deeper discernment of life and faith through his Word.

Wrestling Toward Understanding

For months after our loss, I wrestled quietly with God and kept all my thoughts and doubts to myself as people on the outside spoke into my life. As confused as I was about my beliefs, I never stopped talking to God. Deep down, I knew he was my only way out of the darkness surrounding me. As people in our circles tried to console us, I began to recognize where others had misunderstandings of truth as well.

In the darkest moments of grief, I experienced these conversations as if swimming underwater. I could hear but did not discern the words. I recognized faces but never felt connected. As I came up for air, I heard people telling me I would be fine as a strong person of faith. They had confidence I would behave appropriately in my grief because they could not (or refused to) see my inner battle raging to hold tight to hope. Encountering well-intentioned but empty comments about being young and having other children made me question the validity of my grief. The pressure to be a Christian poster child for strength in the face of loss felt tangible. Living up to this ideal became a heavy and unnecessary burden, compounded by deep sorrow.

Inside, I felt shattered. Blaming God for my bitterness and hurt, I wrestled as Jacob had in the account in Genesis. Frustrated with the way his life had gone, he fought to receive God's blessing. Because I believed wrestling with doubt was sinful, I never expressed this spiritual battle with others. I showed up for church. I sang the songs. I smiled as I went down the hallways. But secretly, I questioned the point of it all.

A Defining Moment

We were youth workers at the time, and one Sunday, a young teenaged girl came into class with a healthy baby cradled in her arms. The floodgate of my sorrow broke. My swirling thoughts landed on Deuteronomy 28 and the covenant (a solemn agreement made between God and man) God had made with the Israelites. In summary, God told them that if they obeyed, they would be blessed; if they disobeyed, they would be cursed.

Believing this as a foundational truth of faith, I allowed bitterness to take root over a young woman's blessing and what felt like a curse upon my life. My sexual purity and desire to pursue Christ felt meaningless in that moment. This tension forced me to consider whether I was experiencing doubt in God's goodness or a clear misunderstanding of biblical truth. I genuinely loved God and sought to serve him with my life, but God had not blessed my efforts. Instead, he had allowed me to endure an inconceivable pain, leading to many nights of seeking and listening.

What had I done wrong? Why didn't God hear and fulfill the desires of my heart? Wasn't this also promised to me in Scripture? Day by day, I wrestled toward understanding.

Reordered Truth

God used this tragedy to draw me closer to the truth. Not the truth as I wanted it to be, but God's truth. The truth is that in this world, we will have trouble. Everyone will experience loss and pain in this fallen world at some point. Jesus said, "I have told you all this so that you may have peace in me. Here on earth you will have many trials and sorrows. But take heart, because I have overcome the world" (John 16:33).

Still, I longed for someone to understand and enter my pain. I needed peace and a reminder to take heart. Thankfully, God cared about my pain. He saw me and invited me into his perfect rest, which came as I spent time seeking him above all else. I remained in this place of rest through believing who he said I was and trusting he was always on my side.

Promises Versus Principles of God

Through the habit of regular Bible study, God taught me that not every passage is a promise for every believer, and not every piece of writing is directly applicable to my life. There are various covenants with different people throughout time. Jesus came to create a new way, or new covenant, for mankind to have peace with God through faith in him alone.

Understanding the Bible is a lifelong journey. All Scripture is useful to teach us what is true and should be carefully studied, but it takes an intimate knowing and enduring faith to understand its mysteries and to develop discernment.

During my time of wrestling, my relationship with God grew beyond a mere cliché. He became life itself, the sustainer of my soul. Through spending time in his presence, I experienced a palpable peace as I learned to discern between universal principles and specific promises of God.

The Covenant of Grace

I was wrong to believe that this young girl's actions disqualified her from receiving blessings from God. Regrettably, God's grace in her life stirred up jealousy in mine. Grace gifted her with something I desperately longed for, and my bitterness judged her harshly. It revealed the ugliness lurking in my heart and mind that needed to be purged and renewed to receive healing.

My battle with grief revealed my misconceptions of the covenants between God and man. When Jesus arrived, he instituted a covenant of grace—a promise of salvation by his work and not ours—accomplishing what the law and Old Testament rules could not. Through faith alone, I am given life and freedom due to the death, burial, and resurrection of Jesus.

Here is the heart of that covenant: "God saved you by his grace when you believed. And you can't take credit for this; it is a gift from God. Salvation is not a reward for the good things we have done, so none of us can boast" (Ephesians 2:8–9).

Reordered Affections

Understanding God's covenant of grace reordered my affections toward truth. Salvation is not a reward for the good things done. I should obey, love, and serve him out of gratitude for all he did to save me. My service should stem from love and not from fear of suffering.

The mercy and grace I receive are not based on what I have done or failed to do. I have nothing to boast about except Christ, deserving no more than anyone else.

While those in Christ live under a covenant of grace, the Bible does teach us that we will benefit from growing and seeking Christ. Suffering can be due to sin in our lives, but as we see in the life of a man named Job, it is not always the case. It was because he was righteous that God allowed him to be tested with all sorts of terrible trials.

All Scripture must be compared with the whole of Scripture. God is not confined to work within a box. The parameters we impose on him are for our purpose in understanding life, not his. God rewards people for their faithfulness but not always in the way we desire. Checking our motivation is the key to understanding this mystery, and my loss forced me to consider my own. Did I desire to receive or to give glory to God?

How Suffering Strengthened my Faith

Growing up in church, I knew about the Bible but had failed to take responsibility for searching the Scriptures on my own. I had filled my mind with what other people thought Scripture said and what traditions of the church were passed on to me without taking personal ownership of my faith.

Explaining most of my convictions and beliefs without cliché phrases proved difficult. It was easier to look to others and copy their decisions instead of depending on God to give me wisdom and direction. However, there is no wisdom or peace apart from God.

God, ever-present, provided peace in my wrestling. According to the Bible, God can bless whomever he chooses. It rains on the just and unjust, and his grace is available to all. Whatever he allows is for his glory and will be used to produce a truer reflection of his glory in my life.

After losing my son, a deep desire to know Christ emerged. Not one that others fed to me, but a personal relationship that shaped my character and actions. I gained compassion and humility where it had lacked. I became entirely dependent on Christ for my very will to live and breathe. Over time, the closeness led to restoration and a discerning spirit. After plunging to these depths, I received rescue and hope in my despair. Experiencing his grace so intimately made it easier to trust him with the daily choices of my life. Through abiding in him, my confidence increased, and my faith flourished.

For the first time, I understood the principle of taking joy in suffering.

Suffering produces character, perseverance, and hope. It brings us to a place where words on a page, great speech from sermons, and cultural platitudes are challenged by truth, and true intimacy and peace are found hidden under the wings of the Almighty God. This is the place where faith and suffering collide and where God reorders our affections and realigns our truths with his.

Renew and Restore

- What moments in your life have revealed a misguided understanding about God?
- What is one misunderstanding you have had of Scripture? How have you worked through it, or how are you currently working through that understanding? Who do you turn to when you aren't sure?
- What is the difference between applying the principles of God found in Scripture to your life versus claiming *all* of the promises of God?
- How has suffering reshaped your character and your trust in God?

Terri Prahl is an aspiring author whose greatest desire is to encourage believers to make every effort to pursue Christ and love Scripture. Terri is an introverted and introspective, creative soul who loves walking in nature, studying Scripture, reading non-fiction, perusing flea markets, and mentoring young women. She writes about her faith journey of resting and wrestling at www.terriprahl.com. She lives in the beautiful Ozark Mountains with her husband and young adult daughter.

Breakdowns to Breakthroughs

Sarah Buckland

If you were to observe a day in my life, you'd conclude that "go-getter" is my middle name. A packed schedule, stacks of books piled high on my desk, and racing thoughts were a part of my typical routine as a full-time postgraduate student and founder and producer of a newly minted online ministry. I was an active presenter at seminars and mulling on an entrepreneurial idea at the same time. My brimful schedule had become a part of who I was. I never thought of it as a distraction, per se, although it had previously functioned as one during my grieving process after my dear grandmother's passing the day before two crucial exams (that's a separate testimony in itself).

Though my goals were clear, in retrospect, my mind wasn't. I often recalled being so utterly exhausted after a day's work that I would lie in bed, literally unable to move a muscle for several minutes. I tried my best to maintain a "balance" in my life. Devotions and connections with God were definitely part of that routine, but what was soon to come showed me that my life's perspective wasn't as balanced and efficient as I'd previously thought.

The Breakdown

My outlook drastically altered on a fine Sunday evening on the seventh of May, 2017. I had a typical day earlier—ministering with my family at elderly homes in the morning, then catching up with some mapwork analysis in preparation for a departmental seminar presentation that was to take place the following week. I had also recently applied for an upgrade from master's to doctorate and was awaiting the confirmation. That night, I went to bed a bit earlier than normal, convincing myself that I was doing a reasonable job at balancing work and just enough self-care. But in a split second, that perspective all changed.

A sudden pressure in my left temple pierced across my brain. My body went into shock mode, and I was convinced that this was a prelude to a stroke. What happened next was like an avalanche. The stabbing sensation echoed from one side of my head to the next for some minutes, then my heartbeat became irregular, and pain raced from my fingers on my left hand. If it weren't for my parents' quick actions of prayers and reassurance, only God knows if I would have lived to proclaim this testimony!

What ensued over the next month was a perpetual weakness that I never before experienced—swinging blood pressures from very low to high, exhaustion at three-minute conversations, and remnant pressures in my head. However, in the midst of my weaknesses, I experienced an amazing irony: my faith in God was forced to dramatically strengthen. On required bed rest, I was no longer the strong go-getter I used to be, in control of my schedules. Lying on my bed for hours gave me a practical lesson of the truth I knew deep down all along: the accolades, the trophies, the degree—none of these have any value when you are unable to do anything.

Thankfully, the ECGs came back normal, the healing process slowly came, and I regained my strength little by little. I was always a student of the Scriptures, but during these moments, the Bible became especially dear to me. Listening to my audio Bible breathed life and hope into my heart, and even after eventually returning to my studies, quiet Scriptural meditation became part of my daily evening routine. In my meditations, I became particularly fond of the Scripture found in Psalm 127:1–2: "Unless the LORD builds a house, the work of the builders is wasted.

Unless the LORD protects a city, guarding it with sentries will do no good. It is useless for you to work so hard from early morning until late at night, anxiously working for food to eat; for God gives rest to his loved ones."

My experience brought a new light to this passage: the only key ingredient that determines lasting success is God. Although I never consciously considered myself self-reliant, I realized I had been carrying a burden that was not mine to bear. This incident realigned my foundations, and God, like the master builder he is, straightened me out.

The Breakthroughs

Fast forward six months after my breakdown ordeals. With a renewed and realigned sense of purpose, less reliant on my efforts, I saw God's mighty hand of reward. With a new deliberate outlook to remove excess tasks from my schedule, logic would have dictated that less effort would yield fewer results, but that was a risk I was willing to take, especially as a convalescent. Upon retrospect, I realized God was not finished teaching me his lessons that year.

Instead of bustling schedules, blessings began to overflow. In a time span of fewer than six weeks, between November to early December, God enabled me to successfully complete my academic upgrade, travel to two countries for a workshop, win a student competition, and be presented with a national level youth award for academics by the Jamaican Prime Minister. All glory be to the Almighty God – great things he has done!

Reflecting on the entire ordeal in the last seven months of 2017, I can attest with complete confidence to the purpose in the pain that God allowed in my life. There is a special peace and power that comes with humble reliance on God. My breakdown gave me a tangible wake-up call that I was not being a good steward of the body he gave me. While maintaining a go-getter outlook is great, honoring God means maintaining the right balance for his glory, not ours, so we can be effective in his service.

Like my testimony, our world today is fast paced—whether you are a stay-at-home parent, student, in ministry, in business, or in all categories. It is easy to omit quiet time with God and rest for our bodies. However, just as a camera picture is blurry when there is excessive motion, there is no perspective as clear as one you receive when you are forced to a halt.

Solomon said it best: "Fear God and obey his commands, for this is everyone's duty" (Ecclesiastes 12:13).

Fearing God means respecting God in obedience and awe of his glory and power. However, this respect is deeper than just routinely acknowledging God's presence. It entails deliberate communing with him and always seeking to realign our purpose and pace with his vision for us. In a world of a "believe in yourself" mantra, it is tempting to believe that you are ultimately in control. But while doing your part is essential, there is a special kind of power in humble surrender to God.

My transformation to balance remains as an ongoing journey, but one thing that will never leave is the lesson to take one day at a time and rely on God's hand—like a potter and clay—to shape my future, no matter how many detours and obstacles come along the way.

Renew and Restore

- There is a common perception that sufferings and pain disprove God's goodness. Think of a time when you experienced some pain or tragedy in which you saw God's hand and purpose. What were some of the breakthroughs you experienced through the trials?
- Sometimes God presses the "pause" button and allows pain into our lives to realign us to his more glorious purpose. When have you experienced this before?
- Think of a time you were trying to "build your own house" (stressing to complete any task) without asking for God's help. What were some emotions that you felt?
- For the next week, meditate on Psalm 127:1–2 and consider making a commitment to ask for God's help before attempting even the smallest of tasks. Note if you feel any difference.

- King David prayed, "Lord, my heart is not proud; my eyes are not haughty. I don't concern myself with matters too great or too awesome for me to grasp.... O Israel, put your hope in the LORD— now and always" (Psalm 131:1–3). Need help surrendering? Start with this prayer:

> Give us a gentle trust in you, O Lord. Build our house and direct our paths. We believe that your Son bore all our griefs and carried all our struggles when he died and was raised again. We rest in your power. We lean on your purposes and promises and wait on your timing. Thank you, that you cause all things to work together for the good of those who love you. Bring breakthroughs to our breakdowns. In Jesus's name, amen.

Sarah Buckland is an award-winning, freelance Jamaican Christian writer with experience spanning technical and creative genres. She is an only child, preacher's daughter, and has been a Christian for over nineteen years. Sarah is also a Spanish language enthusiast, nature-lover, and a doctoral student in geography. Sarah's drive for Christian advocacy has led her to produce her own ministry series (*God's GLOW* web show) aimed at reaching youth with Bible. Over a dozen of Sarah's articles have been published in Jamaica, Trinidad, and Guyana. sarahfaybuckland.wordpress.com

God in My Loneliness

RL Seaton

When we adopted a beautiful blond-haired, crystal-blue-eyed five-year-old boy with non-verbal autism, who was later diagnosed with a mood disorder, we had no idea how our decision would change our lives. But only weeks before, we'd experienced an event that gave us a glimpse. However, I was too astonished in that moment to grasp what it truly meant for us.

To prepare for our son's arrival, my husband, Rick,* and I attended a seminar describing a variety of behavioral methods for working with children with autism, and we invited our best friends to join us. Although we were extremely nervous, we immediately felt a common bond with the other families in attendance. During the first break, my best friend and I chatted as we headed to the restroom. But stepping into line, I noticed an eerie silence.

As I looked around, every woman stood with eyes pasted to the floor as though she had no voice. After returning to our seats, I asked my friend if she noticed. She admitted she had, with an expression that belied concern. It wouldn't take too many months for me to understand why.

Meeting This Little Guy

About three months before the conference, I sat at my friend's kitchen table. As she and I discussed that Rick and I had been offered to adopt a toddler with cerebral palsy, she questioned if adopting a special needs child frightened me. Because of my medical background, I stated the question wasn't if we were afraid, but if it was God's plan.

She then asked, "Does any type of special needs frighten you?"

Without thinking, I replied, "Yes, you know what frightens me? Autism!"

To this day, I don't know why I said it. The only thing I knew about autism was through watching the movie *Rain Man* with Dustin Hoffman.

The following day, we received a call from the adoption agency telling us about a beautiful little boy with autism who needed a family. Remembering my words only the day before, I nervously laughed inside as the director of the adoption agency described John.* Her speech expressed confidence that the only reason his parents were relinquishing him for adoption was they didn't know how to handle him. At the same time, this implied she assumed we would.

Through a series of extraordinary events, despite our fears, we felt God calling us to become John's parents. And despite those fears, we believed the director's words must be true. They just didn't know how to handle him.

We never understand another fully until we've walked in their shoes.

Autism Then

In the late 1990s, research to understand autism was still in its infancy, and the statistics of having a child with autism were about one in one hundred children.

Children with atypical behaviors common to those with more severe autism were viewed as a spectacle. It was, and still is, common for John to garner the stares of others, both old and young. Unfortunately, as he got older, John responded to others' stares with increased behaviors, as he was determined to give them something to stare at. My reaction to his protestations sometimes made *me* the brunt of stares.

Furthermore, the educational system deemed those with nonverbal autism to be mentally retarded and, therefore, unable to understand even rudimentary rules of society. Anti-social behaviors were often overlooked or even encouraged through ignorance. An incident I remember well occurred when John's second-grade special education teacher asked me to watch as she worked with him. It fascinated her that for months John had continually matched the picture symbols for toilet and pool regardless of how many times she corrected him. Convinced John couldn't understand, it never crossed her mind that his consistent matching choices fit well with the fact he'd recently been kicked out of the pool for using it as a toilet one too many times.

Also, most within our church and social circles had never met anyone with autism and so shied away from interacting. And because of their fears, parents most often chose not to correct their children's sometimes cruel responses. I attempted to educate those around us as best I could, but you can't make people change. The more I tried, the further people backed away.

Fear of the unknown is a strong motivator to retreat.

I am very grateful for the way in which our family embraced our little guy, although they lived so far away and often didn't know how to respond to our strange set of circumstances. I'm also eternally grateful for the small core of people who locally supported us through respite, prayer, and practical help. They gave us a gift most special needs families in our situation rarely experience.

Unparalleled Loneliness

Before the adoption, our lives revolved around the ebb and flow of our church family. We both maintained active leadership roles that included an enjoyable social life. Yet not long after the adoption, it became evident our new family was too odd and uncomfortable for many. Many relationships became uncomfortable as people backed away. Social invitations dwindled, and as John's behaviors became increasingly difficult, any social life we had enjoyed was strangled by the strain within and without.

I stopped attending choir practice.

Eventually, I no longer had the energy to volunteer.

In time, we struggled to maintain our only social and spiritual event of the week, the Sunday morning service.

Unfortunately, people got used to missing us. I never got used to missing them.

To fill the void, we began to attend Special Olympics events, as they readily accepted us. It did help to salve some of my wounds, but truthfully, I wasn't ready to accept their culture as my own. I wanted *my* world to accept *my* son. I wrongly assumed that's what you're supposed to do.

Trying to live in two worlds eventually made us citizens of none.

However, no one but God understood my greatest loneliness. I knew I had no clue how to raise John or face our seemingly insurmountable challenges and feared losing him to someone who could do a better job.

At the same time, I was petrified this would be my life forever. So, I determined not to end up like those moms standing in line for the bathroom at the seminar. I refused to look down. Rather, I fought with everything in me to change my world and make it feel safer. We home-schooled John for six years, hired advocates, fought educational labels, and tried to educate the people around us until I no longer had any fight left within me.

Had I only realized there are some battles only God's power can win.

God Wasn't Distant

Especially during the early years as John adjusted to his new life, there were times when without warning, he'd wail uncontrollably. Frustrated that I had no clue what he needed, I would quietly cry out to God for wisdom. Instantly, a thought would enter my mind, and I'd respond to John as though he had spilled his heart out to us, with consoling words fit for the thought God had given me. Instantly he'd stop crying, smile, and go about his activities as though nothing had happened. This happened often enough that when his communication improved, he indicated he thought I'd read his mind. No, we just serve a mighty God.

Over the years, as the storm around and within intensified, there were nights I'd walk around our cul-de-sac screaming out to God like some crazy woman. However, before returning home, God would wash over me his peace and calm as his Spirit ministered to my very wounded soul.

In addition, eight years after adopting John, Rick was diagnosed with cancer. Two years later, before Rick died in 2008, we made the hardest decision of our lives, to place John in temporary foster care through DSS's Voluntary Placement program. As John headed into his teen years, his increasingly difficult behaviors became too much for me to handle, so

Rick had taken over much of John's care. Once Rick was gone, I feared what John and I might do to one another. God provided two angels disguised as social workers to help us navigate the process. It was extremely painful because we loved John, but God kept making a way where there shouldn't have been.

After Rick's death, God provided for each of us a place for respite and healing. John was temporarily moved to another state for needed treatment, and God provided a place and a family who welcomed me when I visited him. A family from our home church had moved to a neighboring community only four years before. When they heard about Rick's death and John's transition, they offered me a place to stay whenever I was in town. Their pastor and his wife also had a son with autism, so the entire church welcomed me heartily. This family and their church's loving ministry brought me the strength I didn't have on my own. Today, because these people willingly became Jesus's hands and feet in my life, I remember that time through the lens of God's amazing love.

After six months of treatment, John was moved back to our home state and into a residential home and school for children with severe behaviors, where I visited him weekly. By the time he turned twenty-one, it was determined he needed twenty-four-hour care, so he now lives comfortably in a permanent residential home with three other men.

In 2012 I remarried. My husband, David,* was also a widow with two adopted sons. Now, as John's stepfather, he has willingly taken on a crucial role in our new uniquely blended family. I am John's legal guardian, and we have a better relationship than we have ever known.

In 2015, John yielded his life to Jesus and asked to be baptized. He is now in his late twenties, and although he still struggles, he seems more at peace with his world. He attends a local church with his fellow residents, where they are welcomed and accepted.

Our family is nothing like it used to be, but it is good. We have all come a long way in our journey from one family to another because God has been so very faithful to navigate our paths as he promised in Romans 8:26–28.

Are your circumstances way beyond what you can bear? You aren't alone. God sees your pain. He hears your cries. Romans 8:26 states that his Spirit within you assists in carrying your load and then cries out to

God on your behalf. Therefore, you can be confident that God's power within and around you is fashioning every difficulty and mess into something beautiful. Wait and see!

*Names have been changed to protect the privacy of the individuals.

Renew and Restore

- How have you experienced the God who is present and powerfully cares? Describe the reassurance you discovered.
- Who else do you know who needs to hear that hope and encouragement? How can you come alongside someone else in their loneliness? Think about the people you know and identify one person whom you can reach out to.
- Read Romans 8:26–39. Make a list of the encouraging hope you find in this passage.

RLSeaton first published this story in a longer format as *Facing Loneliness.* She is a published author, Bible teacher, adversity coach, and speaker who is passionate about sharing God's power in the midst of our struggles. You can find her writings and photography at www.rlseaton.com and on Instagram @rlseaton. Her message is simple: "Jesus invites you to seek him in your adversity. For only in him will you discover life and hope beyond your wildest imaginings."

Phobia to Fearless

Linda L. Kruschke

We have a saying in my family. When someone exhibits an inherited familial trait or habit, we might say, "She comes by it honestly." I didn't learn my fear of water—my aquaphobia—from a family member. It isn't genetic either. But I did come by it honestly.

I grew up in Southern California, and every California kid has to know how to swim. I escaped the scorching California sun by splashing around our three-foot above-ground pool in the backyard or in the shallow end of the local park pool. Concerned for my safety, my mom signed me up for swim lessons in the third grade.

The first thing you learn in swim lessons is how to tread water. Survival depends on staying afloat. I gazed across the sparkling water, rippling from the many kids splashing around, wishing I could head back to my comfort zone in the shallow end. But the instructor told me to slip over the side into the seven-foot end, push away from the edge, and tread water. Easy peasy.

He carefully demonstrated the appropriate arm and leg movements poolside, so all the students could easily see. Anyone can master the simple maneuver. Everyone floats, and this lesson should have been easy.

I followed his instructions perfectly—and sank like a pebble.

I was a skinny little thing back then, with not an ounce of fat and pitiful lung capacity due to living with smokers. I frantically continued to tread water at the bottom of the pool, looking up at the surface where life-sustaining air remained in abundance. Terrified, I couldn't return to the top no matter what I did. Then the lifeguard jumped in and pulled me out.

I don't remember what the lifeguard looked like, even whether a man or a woman. I only remember what it looked like to be struggling helplessly, with over four feet of water between my three-foot frame and the surface. For a long time after that, nightmares regularly interrupted my sleep. I endured many nights trapped underwater with a sheet of glass preventing me from breaching the surface.

My Phobia Manifested

I did eventually learn to swim, but I've never been comfortable in the water. If I ever got in a pool—and I seldom did—I always stayed in the shallow end, and my hair and glasses stayed dry. I dog paddled around where my feet could still touch the bottom.

My loved ones never understood this irrational fear. After all, I didn't actually drown during swim lessons. My husband, Randy, even joked about my dry hair in the pool. My sister wondered what on earth was the matter when I fell off my pool noodle during a water aerobics class. My head went underwater, I panicked, and came up crying hysterically. Even though the five-foot-deep pool presented no real danger, I had to get out and refused to get back in—my last night of water aerobics.

One time, Randy and I vacationed to Eastern Washington. He wanted to rent a boat on Wickiup Reservoir near our campground. The idea did not thrill me, but I agreed to make him happy. The experience proved no fun for either of us. For me, because I remained in panic mode the whole time, sitting in the front of the boat scanning for submerged logs. I felt certain we would hit one and I'd fly out of the boat. For him, because I kept pointing out every submerged log I saw and screaming that he needed to slow down.

Alone at the Zoo

The year our son, Benton, turned ten, our family ventured to Hawaii. Unlike me, Benton has zero fear of water. He would have ignored the high surf warning signs on the beach if we'd let him. I agreed to let him participate in a dolphin experience at our hotel on the Big Island. He barely contained his excitement, but they had no spots open before our scheduled flight to Oahu.

Randy did some research and discovered a snorkeling trip off of Oahu for the following week. The description said it involved swimming with spinner dolphins. He wanted to book it for the three of us, but I almost had a panic attack just thinking about it. I refused to get out of a boat in the middle of the ocean, even to see a beautiful coral reef.

"You two just go," I insisted.

"You could stay in the boat," he replied.

Yeah, that wasn't going to work either.

While Randy and Benton swam with spinner dolphins, watching colorful Hawaiian fish and holding an octopus, I meandered around the Honolulu Zoo. I love zoos, but not alone.

The next day, they convinced me to join them on a sunset catamaran tour. While Benton hung out on the nets at the front of the boat and Randy videotaped his antics, I cowered in a corner in the back, trying not to imagine the boat capsizing and drowning us all.

I missed out on the snorkeling trip with its cool tropical fish, octopus, spinner dolphins, and more. I missed out on witnessing Benton's joy on the catamaran. Simply because of fear.

Praying to Overcome

Ten years later, Randy and I planned a trip to Maui. A determination to redeem what I had lost on that first trip overwhelmed me. I felt a strong desire to snorkel and witness the beauty of God's underwater creation. I knew I needed more than my paltry supply of courage to overcome decades-long aquaphobia.

Four months before the trip, I started my prayer campaign. I petitioned several groups of friends to pray specifically that I would overcome my fear and snorkel. I asked my sisters-in-law, my Bible Study Fellowship leaders' group, and my friends at church. I prayed every day that God would give me the courage to experience a successful and enjoyable adventure. I wanted to snorkel, but I first had to conquer this aversion to swimming in the deep.

On our first day on the island, we rented snorkel equipment for the week, including prescription goggles so I could see what teemed below the water's surface. In the Westin Hotel pool, I stood in three and a half feet of water and donned my snorkel mask as Randy lounged poolside, patiently waiting for me to put my face in the water and swim. We couldn't snorkel Black Rock if I couldn't master breathing through a snorkel tube in this relatively calm environment. He chuckled and snapped pictures as I flapped my lower arms up and down, trying to drum up the nerve to breathe underwater.

I succeeded!

God is good. He answered my prayer in ways I never imagined. I later realized God had begun answering my prayer many years earlier. The night I met Randy, long before I knew it would be my prayer, God knew I would need more than courage—I would need encouragement. So, he brought Randy to hold my hand through the experience.

Swimming with the Fishes—Literally

The next day—on my birthday—I snorkeled Black Rock just down the beach from our hotel with Randy holding my hand. We paddled around together, observing the fish. He continued to hold my hand as long as I needed him to. He pointed to a beautiful eel in the reef, and I motioned toward a brightly colored school swimming below us. We ventured much farther out from the beach together than I ever would have alone.

The one downside of Black Rock for snorkeling is that people frequently jump off the cliffs from above, and they aren't terribly careful about where they land. At one point, someone jumped in, landing two feet from me, and I got water in my snorkel. I started to panic, but then I remembered and recited one of my favorite verses—"Do not be anxious about anything, but in every situation, by prayer and petition, with thanksgiving, present your requests to God. And the peace of God, which transcends all understanding, will guard your hearts and your minds in Christ Jesus." (Philippians 4:6–7 NIV)—and God's supernatural peace calmed my heart. I resumed my snorkeling and thanked him for the beautiful underwater scenery and creatures he had created for me to enjoy.

When I wanted to get out of the water after only a short swim that first day, Randy didn't give me a hard time but understood and swam to shore with me. Although we cut our first snorkel short, we ventured out three more times during the week. We took a guided boat tour one day, and I fearlessly snorkeled on my own around Honolua Bay and Honokohau Bay while Randy SNUBA snorkeled with an instructor. I encountered *humuhumunukunukuapua'a* (Hawaiian triggerfish), octopuses, huge sea turtles, *lauwiliwili nukunuku 'oi'oi* (longnose butterflyfish), spotted eels, yellow butterflyfish, and more.

On later trips to Hawaii, I've marveled at the beauty of God's underwater creation at Molokini Crater, Kapalua Bay, Hanauma Bay (Oahu), and on the island of Lanai. What began as a timid attempt to simply float face down in a hotel pool turned into a lifetime of savoring the charm of reef life. I can't wait to find the next reef or bay to snorkel. My new fearless passion inspired this peaceful haiku:

> Relaxing in waves
>
> Sun dappled reef and fish
>
> What season? Who cares

Any season is ripe for a fearless experience. God's peace truly comes to us in the deep—I can't explain how—when we pray with thanksgiving for the blessings he has in store for us.

The Blessings of Fearlessness Abound

The fearless life doesn't end at the shore. It permeates everything I do and everything I write. "God has not given us a spirit of fear and timidity, but of power, love, and self-discipline" (2 Timothy 1:7). If I begin to fear, I remember the reef and the spotted eel. I recall how God provided all I needed to overcome my aquaphobia and swim fearlessly with a kaleidoscope of sea life.

Song lyrics from one of my favorite Christian bands reveal how we often have deep-water faith but stay in the shallow end of life. What a perfect metaphor for my life. Fear kept me from taking hold of the abundant life that God had in store for me. I had deep-water faith but also intense fear of deep water. Thanks to prayer and God's faithfulness, I could completely surrender and be immersed in the Holy Spirit, trusting that I needn't fear the deep end because Jesus will always stay with me.

Renew and Restore

- What is your biggest fear, and how did it originate?
- Who can you invite into your prayer circle to overcome this fear?
- What would your life look like if you could approach each day without paralyzing fear?
- Describe how it feels to overcome a phobia.

Linda L. Kruschke writes candid memoir and fearless poetry and delves into hard issues others tend to avoid. She aspires to show women that God's redemption and healing are just a story away. If she could spend every moment talking or writing about Jesus, she would. She blogs at AnotherFearlessYear.net and AnchoredVoices.com and has been published in *Fathom Magazine, The Christian Journal, Bible Advocate, iBelieve.com, WeToo.org blog, The Mighty,* and several anthologies.

When Grace Rewrites Your Story

Maureen Cresencia Kambarami

 t was the same high-pitched scream all the time, as it had been for years, and each time I heard my own cries in my memories, I cringed in pain.

"Mummy! Mummy!

"Daddy! Daddy please . . . Daddy stop!

"Mummy! Mummy . . ."

Genesis

The pain, suffering, and desperation that filled the whole room was overbearing, and no matter how hard I tried, I could never block the sound of fists bumping against flesh. God knows, I would have given anything in the world to erase that chapter of my life, even inducing amnesia, for the whole scenario left me sick all the time.

"Here, try to drink some water. It will cool you down. You had that dream again. I really wish you would talk about it. Maybe that way, the dreams will stop," my friend Rachel said as she helped me to sit up.

"I told you that when I wake up, I don't remember a thing. It isn't like

I'm hiding something. One day when I remember, you will be the first to know."

Rachel looked at me, accurate disbelief in her eyes, but I didn't care. That was my secret. Yes, I knew not talking about it was foolish. It was like drinking poison and expecting my enemies to die, but I had no other option.

"Then, maybe, you must seriously consider going for therapy. You can't go on like this."

"You're right. I will consider it. But for now, can I just sleep? Please!"

"Ok, ok, but whenever you need to talk, remember I am here. You don't need to suffer in silence."

I turned over and let out a pretentious yawn so Rachel would drop the subject, but my mind refused to be bluffed. Sleep only engulfed me at daybreak.

It was many years later when I considered therapy. At first, it was out of curiosity, but with time, something happened, which made me write this story of hope, forgiveness, and acceptance. A story that shows that when God's grace locates you, it has the power to turn trash into gold.

Egypt

I grew up so embarrassed that my very first memories on this earth, which date back to when I was approximately five years old, were about domestic violence. There were times when I really wished I could erase these memories because I could not disclose to anyone how my father used to beat up my mother after every drinking spree and how I would scream my lungs out in the hope that he would either stop or someone would come.

However, it was the same pattern every time. No matter how hard I screamed, no one came. And my father didn't stop. Instead, we became nomads, frequently getting chased away from our rental abode for the noise, 90 percent of which was my fault. I grew up with that guilt haunting me in my sleep. No wonder I had frequent nightmares.

Physical abuse was not my father's only problem; he was also verbally abusive. He made it no secret that he preferred a son to a daughter, and he put me down every chance he got, calling me names. I always paid for school stuff at the last minute because "educating a girl was a waste of money," as girls became prostitutes when they got older anyway. As a result, I grew up with low self-esteem, and I believed that I was ugly and unlovable.

Despite the toxicity in my parents' marriage and the long string of affairs my father indulged in, my mother stayed in that sham of a marriage for fourteen years, her reason being that she wanted us to have a better life and she was unemployed.

Exodus

When my mother finally decided to leave her marriage, I was overjoyed because I thought I would finally experience a normal childhood like my peers. Little did I know what was in store for me. I was sent to live with my grandmother in a remote rural village where I became grandchild number ten.

The sad reality about living in rural Zimbabwe was that the things I had previously thought were necessities were actually luxuries because of poverty. For instance, cooking oil was a luxury that we only got once or twice a year. For the greater part of our lives, we ate dried vegetables without any oil. Occasionally, we would grind roasted nuts and make peanut butter soup, and when this happened, it was an early Christmas for us. At first, the dried vegetables without cooking oil tasted like rubber in my mouth, but with time, I got used to the taste and tolerated enough mouthfuls to ensure my stomach did not growl at night.

Toiletries were hard to come by, and as such, we did a lot of improvisation. For instance, washing powder could be substituted by a certain soapy plant, which we crushed and rubbed on the dirty clothes. Sanitary towels could be substituted with old pieces of cloth or blankets, and we took pride in choosing the type of material and designs we wanted. Body lotion could be substituted by either cooking oil or washing soap, and when we were really stranded, we rolled peanut butter into a small ball, mixed it with water, and rubbed the oil on our bodies.

The walk to and from school was no child's play. It was approximately ten kilometers (6.2 miles), and therefore, I lost a lot of weight. After school, I also had to do heavy chores, such as fetching water or firewood, on an empty stomach before cooking the evening meal. Homework was done late at night by candlelight, or I had to leave home around 4:00 a.m. so that I could do my homework at school before teaching commenced. However, despite all these hardships, I was always at the top of my class. With time, I went to college and scored a good job upon completion.

Canaan

When I started working, I blocked my past and moved on with my life. However, it would irritatingly creep into my relationships with the opposite sex when I least expected it. I got involved with the wrong people because I thought no one could ever love me. I was nearly sexually violated twice by gangster boyfriends (with whom I should never have become involved in the first place). It was as if I was a magnet that attracted only the wrong men.

I later met a guy who promised me heaven on earth, while inwardly he was a wolf in sheep's clothing. He forced me to have an abortion, and when I refused, he became abusive and openly dated other women in revenge. Ironically, I did not leave the relationship even though I had crucified my mother so many times for doing the same. I stayed in this loveless and lethal relationship because I was scared to be alone. When I finally broke ties with him, I went on a downward spiral of destruction. I was like a train without brakes.

I joined an online dating site not to find love but for revenge. I then had countless casual affairs meant to make me feel good, but instead, they added to the emptiness I felt inside. I had a deeper longing for satisfaction, and I was very unhappy, even though I had all the material possessions in the world. I survived two attempts on my life as a result of a relationship with a narcissist, and it was at this point that I finally woke up from my slumber. I knew that I had to change my lifestyle, so I decided to go for therapy.

At first, I was skeptical and told the therapist that I would not commit for a long time. I still laugh at the way I introduced myself during the first session, telling the therapist I knew exactly what was wrong with me and doubted that there was anything new she could tell me, but she was welcome to try.

After a couple of sessions, I got in touch with myself and learned to love the real "me" unconditionally. I broke down all my defenses and faced my childhood pain, hurts, disappointments, and fears. I also faced my anger because, for a long time, I hated my father for all the pain and misery he caused us as a family through the way he treated my mother and me. I also hated my mother for staying in an abusive marriage for over a decade.

I harbored so much anger stemming from my traumatic childhood, and this anger, like a cancer, gradually devoured me. It is through therapy that I realized how much this anger affected my personal relationships and stole my joy.

The Metamorphosis

When I finally decided to let go of my anger, that's when I truly understood what Jesus meant when he said, "But I say, love your enemies! Pray for those who persecute you! (Matthew 5:44). The conscious decision to forgive my father was not an easy one, but it was a necessary part of my healing. Forgiving what you cannot change or forget is strenuous. Even though I confronted my father looking for answers, I got none. However, talking to him was cathartic because for the first time in my life, I could tell him how I felt as a child and how his behavior had impacted my self-esteem.

True forgiveness is neither a once-off affair nor an honorary medal but is a continuous process. Each day, I make a conscious effort to focus on the present and the positives and not dwell on the past, which I cannot change. Believe me, if I could, I would change my history, but since it's impossible, I have chosen to embrace it. I now love my past because it taught me to be a better person. I now know what true forgiveness is because of past hurts, and I know what love is because I learned to love myself unconditionally and take care of my inner self.

Opening up about my childhood trauma was the best decision I ever made in my life, for it took away all the embarrassment, shame, and guilt that had been my cloak for years—the cloak that hid a beautiful "me," a woman who has inspired countless women to be the best version of themselves through motivational talks and counseling.

When I look back at my life, I just see the hand of God lifting me out of the miry clay (Psalm 40:2), and I know I am a better person today than I was yesterday, perfected by the trials and tribulations I experienced. Above all, I know that I am beautiful, lovable, and worthy to be loved because God does not create trash. I have a better relationship with my father now, and I no longer blame my mother for my pain.

Above all, I am free, no longer a slave to anger, bitterness, and resentment. When I finally opened up my heart to love again, after the painful metamorphosis, God blessed me with the right partner, a man who understands my journey and feels honored to be a part of it. I will forever be grateful for my painful path, which transformed my junk into treasure.

Renew and Restore

- Which part of your childhood do you find hard to accept and why?
- Sometimes we make poor choices while searching for love and acceptance. Describe how it feels to know that Jesus offers unconditional love, grace, and acceptance to you.
- Look back at your life to a moment when you struggled with forgiveness. How did you manage to move on? What advice would you give to someone in the same situation?
- Psalm 40:2 says, "He lifted me out of the pit of despair, out of the mud and the mire. He set my feet on solid ground and steadied me as I walked along." Describe what it means to you to be lifted out of despair and set on solid spiritual and emotional ground.

Maureen Cresencia Kambarami is a social worker from South Africa with extensive experience in family counseling and therapy. A woman after God's Word and principles, she is passionate about writing Christian articles and believes in telling authentic stories to inspire and uplift others.

All I Have Are Dry Bones

Amy Mein

I *keep thinking that the next* chapter of my life is the one where things work themselves out. *That's* when I figure out problem A. *That's* when problem B is no longer problematic. *That's* when this person or that person starts—or stops—the thing that's going to finally bring peace.

I've nominated myself to the gifted-and-talented "next chapter" program as a parent. I keep waiting for when the child starts walking. Or when they start school. Or when they get their driver's license. I don't want to brag, but I'm pretty good at not living in the moment.

I seem to also be pretty skilled at having a career path that looks a wee bit like a funnel cake rather than anything linear. As I'm typing this, there's an upcoming job choice to make in the next day or two that, hopefully, will look less like a fun fair confection and more like moving on to the next natural step.

Admittedly, the struggles in my life have not been on par with true hardship stories. But no matter the size of the challenges we might face, one thing we commonly share is the enormity of how the obstacle in front of us *feels*. It'd be great to declare that I'm always tackling things with God at the forefront of my decision-making process, but far too often, I find myself trying to figure things out or using logic to solve an equation that can't be solved by logic alone.

That's not to say that there haven't been legitimate challenges along the way. Emotional, financial, and medical difficulties have risen up in my path. Those seem easier to identify when faith has to kick in. When your husband is diagnosed with a spinal problem that could mean life-long paralysis, those warning signs are easy to understand. "Oh, this is bigger than me! I'm a person of faith so naturally I cry out to God to intervene." The giant, flashing, neon-road-signs-flavor of warnings are super easy for me to spot and respond appropriately.

The signs that are harder for me to spot are the issues that zap my energy over weeks and months and years until all I have left are these dry bones. It's a feeling of weariness, yes, but also just cracked, dry, nothing left to give, and if anyone asks for just one more thing, I'm likely to crumble into a million pieces and blow away in the wind. Wouldn't it be super to say that I notice and identify when I start to feel just a little dehydrated and immediately look to my support system—and my Support System—to quickly remedy the problem? Well, that's not been my history. I have a little more stubborn ox-ness in me.

Sun-Bleached Skeletons

My mom and I have noticed that when we're together for extended periods of time, we pretty quickly recognize that when we feel sluggish or out of sorts (or unduly tired on shopping trips because we're not shopaholics), we're both thinking, *Wow, why am I so tired?*

It doesn't take long for one of us to voice, "Oh, we must hydrate!" and then we quickly find something to quench the thirst.

But dry bones, sometimes they're all I have. My most recent emptiness was similar to what Ezekiel talked about in the Old Testament. He saw a vision of a valley of bones all around, and they were dry, lifeless, and bleached by the sun. God told Ezekiel to talk to the bones and that (God) would make breath enter the bones so that they could come to life.

But it wasn't a one-step process. First, Ezekiel did as commanded, and the bones took skeletal structure and had muscle and skin restored. But there was no breath in them. In step two, Ezekiel followed God's further instruction to "now speak to the breath."

The Lord tells him to say, "Come, O breath, from the four winds! Breathe into these dead bodies so they may live again" (Ezekiel 37:9).

I admit it feels a little creepy to think about being there and witnessing such a scene. Pretty confident that I'd be in full freak-out mode watching bones assemble and seeing flesh added to formerly lifeless things. It's different than singing "the hip bone's connected to the leg bone" as we did in grade school.

What does give me hope is that I can feel my most weary, most stretched thin, and at the brink of giving up, and that's exactly when God wants to speak to my breath. He doesn't want my hope lost but to restore the hope I so desperately need.

He calls the breath from the four winds to restore me. The four winds! Not just a tiny poof of a breath, but all corners of the earth.

Singing Stones

While this could just sound like a story about depression and hope after depression, I think there's more to it. There's another part of the Bible that talks about stones crying out (Luke 19:40). However, it isn't just the stones or rocks that cry out. The hills break forth in singing, and trees clap their hands (Isaiah 55:12). Interesting. Tree hands. I'd like to see that someday.

Sun, moon, stars, highest heavens, and waters above the heavens praise the Lord (Psalm 148). If sun, moon, and stars are doing something that resembles hand clapping or celebrating, I'd also pay money to see whatever that looks like.

The next step starts by bringing my dry bones with me. I feel spent, out of energy, much like the valley of dry bones. My quest for the breath that's promised starts with hope. And it's not always a gigantic mountain of hope. Sometimes I'm the rock crying out, and other times I'm standing next to the rock, crying because I didn't cry out. Or couldn't.

I've been a Christian for longer than I can remember, and that's afforded me both the opportunity to watch people do things the right way and also probably more opportunities to observe people of faith doing things the wrong way. Well-meaning people (mostly), but there's a key principle that can sometimes be easily overlooked. You may have seen the WWJD bracelets (What Would Jesus Do) from years ago, and those are excellent reminders of trying to act in a moment with honor. But I recently saw the answer to that question on a different bracelet—and it was spelled out as HWLF. *He Would Love First.* That smacked me between the eyes.

Regardless of how long I've been a Christian, I screw up royally and often, and I think that's pretty normal for humans. But my hope comes in the fact that when I mess up, HWLF. He (God/Jesus/Holy Spirit) would love me first, care for my basic needs, and then later bring the loving correction. He has full rights to call me an idiot when I'm being an idiot, but instead, he fills me with hope first, fills me with breath before anything else.

Breath Restored

If I want to understand what Jesus would do, then I have to first love others—no matter their political view, religious beliefs, cultural differences, hatred toward me, or any other type of strife or disagreement we may have. First comes love, in order to respond with valor in any situation.

All I have are these dry bones. But that's the point. If we had it all figured out, then life would be a breeze. The first step is to continue to bring these dry bones, anticipating that much-needed breath. But the second step—gaining back breath—is where we're fulfilled to allow us to move forward, even if that first breath is a huge inhale because of oxygen deprivation.

If you have ever felt like dry bones, know that HWLF. He would love you first, restore that breath that you need in order to see you step into the next chapter in full health. Gasp if you must, but open wide and take in that first breath.

Renew and Restore

- Describe a time in your life when you felt bone-tired and weary.
- If you experienced a defining moment when you felt life and breath restored to you, how did that feel?
- If you're still in a dry valley emotionally, imagine yourself being filled with breath. What do you think you'd be able to accomplish if you were at full-breath capacity?
- Whether or not you are a person of faith, what do you think of the idea of loving first before acting? Would this be an easy principle to incorporate or more of a challenge for you?

Amy Moin lives in Wisconsin with her family and enjoys turning day-to-day weirdness into humor.

A Threadbare Christmas

Tracey Lynn Russell

The night before I moved home to Florida, my cousin's husband called to tell me she was deteriorating rapidly. She'd fought a good fight against cancer for over three years. Worn down from the chemo, the surgeries, and the tumors that still appeared in her body, life was fading from her once sparkling eyes. On a mission, following my plane ride the next day, I drove immediately to see her one last time—to say goodbye.

Walking into her house, I noticed the blinds pulled, the sterile scent, and the heaviness in the air. Through deep breaths and fragmented words, I heard her say, "love . . . you!" She also managed to say, "The pajamas were . . . amazing!"

I had sent her a new pair of satin pajamas in navy blue so she could feel luxurious in her bed. The hospice bed looked far from cozy as she lay painfully contorted and unrecognizable to me. In a surreal moment, I told her I loved her too, and I would see her soon—as she faded into murmurs.

She passed away on a hot summer evening in Florida, with all of her family surrounding her.

The sunset blazed multi-colors in honor of her that night as I silently looked at the sky. Like so many other canceled events, no formal funeral would proceed because of COVID-19. No family gatherings that mark moments of significance in time. A beautiful story abandoned with no ending.

Delayed Grief

For months, I would pass by the bereavement cards at the grocery store. Every time I tried to buy one, I would put it back. *I'll buy that card later*, I would think to myself. *That card is just not right.* I couldn't bring myself to send them to her family just yet.

Without a final funeral for our family, I delayed the real grief. I resisted the sorrow and the sadness of not getting to see her. I fooled myself into believing I would see her at Christmas, like every other year.

Then, the news came that my family was canceling our Christmas Eve tradition due to COVID-19. I shattered. She won't be coming to Christmas this year, and neither will I! Worn down from the losses, the cancelations, and the disappointments of this year, I just sat in my room and felt an emptiness enter my soul.

No Marianne? No family? No Christmas? The phases of grief marched in unexpectedly. Denial, anger, bargaining, and all. With nothing left to look forward to, I began to cry. I pulled up Marianne's Facebook and remembered her final wishes were to send money to The Ballard House, the home where she had stayed while receiving treatment.

One Last Gift

The Ballard House is near Houston, Texas. It's a place where families can live for free while going through medical hardships. The care community here gives so much comfort to those who would never be able to afford living expenses in another state while receiving treatment. The unseen costs of cancer are exorbitant!

A monetary number came to mind immediately, almost as if I were listening to the sound of a voice whispering in my ear. I called her husband just to make sure this is what they wanted. He confirmed that, yes,

Marianne wanted all money to go to The Ballard House instead of having people send flowers or any gifts.

This time last year, I was sending her fuzzy socks. I never imagined I would be sending her funeral money to the same home this year. I picked up the phone to call the director of The Ballard House. An impersonal voicemail greeted me. I left a message with the dollar amount that our family wanted to give. Somehow, the pain in my heart did not ease, as her loss felt unnoticed once again.

Divine Provision

A few days before Christmas, I received a personal call back from the director.

"Mrs. Russell, I have seen God do this before, but I want to share with you what just happened. The day before you called us, we were in a staff meeting about fundraising demands. Due to COVID-19, we were not able to raise any money for a very special need. You see, all our blankets and our sheets are threadbare, and we need to replace them for the residences. The amount you are donating is exactly the amount to make sure all the residents will have new blankets and cozy beds for Christmas this year."

My heart began to feel refreshed at the goodness of God to use what seemed like a last-ditch effort at grief and turn it into a miraculous divine provision for so many in need. Before I could speak a word, the director made me an offer that surprised me like an unexpected gift from heaven.

"Mrs. Russell, we would like to give naming rights to a room here in the Ballard House in memory of your cousin. We'd like to have a plaque made over the door of a room . . . The family will be sent pictures of the room, and we hope that you will pray for the new residents and their time in The Ballad House. It gives our new residents comfort to know that another family has shared their experience. Just let us know what words you would like to say on the plaque, and we will have that made right away!"

All I could say was thank you as I hung up the phone. I know in my heart that God found a way for me to see that my cousin's life was marked with significance. Her life mattered not just to me but to a God who notices every human life as his precious creation. I was so blessed to share the news with her family, and they were brought to tears with the kindness of this unexpected memorial.

You see, our threadbare moments can become woven into the story of others who are threadbare too. The pain of our loss can be transformed into powerful actions that can restore hope for many. Scripture says it best, "For our present troubles are small and won't last very long. Yet they produce for us a glory that vastly outweighs them and will last forever!" (2 Corinthians 4:17).

Renewed Joy for the Season

In making that donation, I felt my first wave of joy in this season and connection to my cousin's memory of being with me at Christmas. With every heartache, we have a God who is unfolding a plan of grace and love for his people.

Christmas is the hope that every threadbare moment that feels as if we are falling apart on the outside can be transformed into a new life on the inside. Jesus's birth is proof that worn-down places can become spaces for miracles when God is present. Worn-down people can be renewed within by the eternal perspective of heaven coming to earth. We have joy and hope to give amid missed family moments.

Maybe you are feeling threadbare too? May your Christmas—and every day—be woven back together with the spirit of God's unfolding grace within your heart.

Renew and Restore

- Can you remember a time you felt a little threadbare, like you were falling apart? How did you cope?
- In what ways have you seen God's grace unfold to you in those threadbare moments?
- Describe how sorrow has overwhelmed you in unexpected moments if you have ever tried to delay grief. What has helped you process the sadness?
- How have you found new hope and joy when your holiday traditions or family plans have needed to change because of some circumstance?
- Name one way you can bless others from an experience when you felt worn down.

Tracey Lynn Russell is a story inspired author, speaker, and coach. She is the founder of The Art of My Story coaching groups that help women discover their story, determine their passion, and direct their influence. You can always find her at *The Heart of the Story* podcast with Tracey Lynn Russell on iTunes or blogging at traceylynnrussell. com. You will rarely find her at the grocery store, much to her family's dismay.

Called to Choose

Natalie Lavelock

s a leaf senses the subtle change of the wind, so, too, was my soul sensing a stir. As I sat at my desk in nursing administration, staring at the skylight, trying to feel the calming warmth of that single ray of light descending into my office, I could feel conflict arising within. It was an unsettled stirring that seemed to be signaling a change on the horizon.

At first, I didn't understand. What was God trying to tell me? I mean, by all external measures, life was good. My family was happy and healthy, I was near the top of the corporate ladder at work. I had the trust and respect of both the hospital administrators and my colleagues who worked at the bedside. What was there to change?

As the unsettled feeling persisted, I noticed myself growing more and more frustrated that everyone around me was content with the status quo. I caught myself saying things like, "Is this all there is?"

"What have I done wrong, Lord? I'm not helping anyone here anymore. I feel as if I'm being shoved under a bushel and my light is growing dim."

You see, I was used to being an earth shaker and a change maker. The administrators of the hospital had grown to trust that I had the best interest of the organization and our patients at heart and that I would make any endeavor we embarked upon successful. But for the past several months, every idea I had was met with a no.

I felt as if I were trapped in the hallway of an old, abandoned apartment building, rattling every door I came to, trying to find one that would open. But the doors were all locked and boarded. And after months and months of trying, I began to lose hope. I felt lost, abandoned, forsaken, and I was afraid God no longer had a purpose for me.

The Storm

A few months later, the announcement came that the hospital CEO and the chief nursing officer (CNO) had decided to retire. Despite how I had been feeling, they were an incredible team to work for. Lynne, my CNO, was not only an exceptional leader but had become a mentor to me over the past couple of years. So, when they announced their retirement, I was both elated for them and heartbroken for me. This must have been what I felt coming those several months ago.

Wrong!

Shortly after that, the new CNO was hired, and within just a couple of weeks, my boss said she wanted to have a meeting. I didn't perceive this to be a big deal. We had regular meetings all the time. It was no secret she was hoping I would take her position as the director of women's services for the hospital when she retired.

But on that day, her whole demeanor was different. As she walked into my office and sat down next to me, I could see the distress on her face. She said, "I have something I have to tell you, something I've been dreading for weeks, and I hope you'll consider my offer."

Wait. What? "What are you telling me, and what offer?"

She proceeded to tell me that the new CNO had decided to eliminate my role within the organization as the clinical nurse educator. But they wanted me to move into a management position to assist my boss in her role running multiple departments.

I wasn't quite sure how to feel, other than shocked at first. I was just trying to sort out the words I had just heard come out of her mouth.

And then, on the one hand, I started thinking of all the things I had done for the organization: creating a new revenue-generating service line, fast-tracking a four-year-long accreditation process to become the fourth hospital in our state to achieve a global designation, developing a nurse residency program to decrease staff turnover, not to mention all of the staff training and patient education programs. *And they're just done with my role?*

Then, on the other hand, I was elated because management *was* the next rung on the ladder and was finally within my reach—what an honor! She then proceeded to tell me that I had the weekend to think about it, but she needed an answer by Tuesday (it was Labor Day weekend, and no one would be working on Monday). I'm not sure whether my sarcastic laugh was fully contained as I thought, *No rush, you know. Just make a quick little decision on something that is going to change the ENTIRE trajectory of my life in seventy-two hours!* The only thing I can remember muttering to her in that moment was, "I'll think about it."

As I left work that day, I wasn't sure whether I wanted to skip and cheer and praise the Lord or cry all the way to my car. But then I started thinking about what this new role would mean for my family.

Having worked for this organization for over fifteen years, I knew the ins and outs of most of the administrative roles. At one point, I thought to myself, *Oh man, this means a new title and a raise! I've waited for this for so long. What a blessing! But then, it also means more time away from my family, being on call 24/7/365, getting called in to work on holidays, nights, and weekends when there is a hole in the staffing schedule. Even after working a 40-plus-hour week.*

And all of a sudden, this "promotion" opportunity felt more like a death trap! I had three little boys at home, who were a precious gift from God. And I only had a short time with them to do the job that no one else could ever do—be their momma. And that began to tug at every string in this momma's heart.

The Gift of Choice

What choice did I have, really? Quit my job?

My family and I headed to the lake for Labor Day weekend, but the decision at hand weighed heavy on my heart. That entire weekend I fasted and prayed, trying to discern what God wanted me to do. And believe me, I felt as though *I was* in labor that Labor Day weekend! As I wrestled with the decision to be made, Satan took the opportunity to create as much confusion and fear as possible. He messed with my thoughts.

Are you really going to throw your career away?

What kind of mother would put her children at risk? No income, no insurance, no retirement.

You're going to lose your home, and your children are going to starve.

Your children are going to hate you.

*Do you **really** think your marriage is strong enough to handle this?"*

And yet, the whole time, I heard God saying, "You get to choose. You can choose prestige—the safety and security of a job—or you can choose to step out in faith and follow me. You can learn to depend on me and watch what I will do."

Let me tell you, that weekend was excruciating!

Seconds seemed like hours, and every decision felt as if it were life or death. And yet, I kept hearing God say, "You get to choose. This is your opportunity. I am with you."

As I was reading my Bible searching for an answer, I came across this verse:

> Then David continued, "Be strong and courageous, and do the work. Don't be afraid or discouraged, for the LORD God, my God, is with you. He will not fail you or forsake you. He will see to it that all the work related to the Temple of the LORD is finished correctly." (1 Chronicles 28:20)

In that moment, I sensed God speak to my heart that I need not fear the decision at hand. That he would be with me because he was building something new, and my job was to simply choose to follow him and then do the work. And in that moment, I knew that everything I had, all of my gifts, skills, and talents, were his to use as he saw fit and that he was simply moving my work to another location where I could shine his light again. That my hospital career had been a training ground for something bigger he wanted to accomplish, and that my location was not as important as my devotion and willingness to be used to achieve his purposes.

With that, the only remaining question was: what was I going to choose?

Even If

In that moment, I knew one thing to be true. I wasn't going to let fear rob me of the opportunity to follow God and experience the goodness of what he had in store—even if it meant walking away from every comfort and security I thought I had. Even if it meant going through financial hardship for a season. And even if it meant I could lose everything. I would trust and follow him, *even if*. Because "even if" is still the safest place to be if it lands you in the arms of Jesus.

So, with all the courage and faith I could muster, I walked into that hospital on Tuesday morning, shaking all the way, and told them I would be resigning my position and I would not be accepting the offer to move into the management position. I won't lie. That was one of the hardest decisions of my life because it affected not only me but three innocent little boys who would have to live with the consequences of my decision.

A New Assignment

You know what? God is good!

He has provided for our family over and over. When things were tough, he always came through, helping us make ends meet as I transitioned into entrepreneurship. I'm learning to trust him with all of my heart and be at peace in walking through fire if that's what he needs me to do to accomplish his purpose.

In the time since choosing to step out in faith and follow his calling, I've been blessed to build a successful educational design company that allows me to use my expertise to help other professionals build training programs and online courses that make a bigger impact in the lives of those they are called to serve. And I get to do it while also doing the most important job I will ever have—being a mom.

But it never would have been possible if I had chosen comfort and security above stepping out in faith to do what felt like the unimaginable and the impossible.

I'm here to encourage you that you can do it too. Whatever that big scary thing is that you're being called to do, you can choose to yes to walking in faith and see for yourself the miracle of what God will do!

Renew and Restore

- In what way might God be trying to repurpose the gifts, talents, and skills he gave to you?
- Are you willing to step out in faith, *even if*? What will that look like for you?
- Pray and ask God to give you the wisdom and courage to trust him in all things, with all your heart.

Natalie Lavelock RN-MSN, founder and CEO of Natalie Lavelock Coaching & Consulting, is a sought-after program development specialist and online business strategist with over fifteen years of experience specializing in program development and professional training. She works with coaches, speakers, and health professionals who *know* they can be making a bigger impact but don't have the training products to make that happen. Connect with Natalie today to create programs with impact! Natalie@ NatalieLavelock.com

Like New, But Better

Daphne Tarango

My self-worth issues sprouted before I was five. I was born left-handed, but due to old wives' tales about how lefties link to the devil, relatives forced me to write with my right hand. I also felt too dark around lighter-skinned relatives. No one said or did anything specifically, but I felt different and less desirable. Around that time, a babysitter introduced me to soap operas, where I learned I could do things to be loved. My five-year-old mind connected those two beliefs and concluded the best way to get acceptance and love was to perform.

My family loved me—of that, I have no doubt. We spent a lot of time together. My parents took us everywhere they went, even to work sometimes. If my brother and I weren't at school, we were at church or at activities such as girl scouts or little league baseball. I loved fishing and eating smoked mullet while we waited for fish to bite. And our ice cream adventures. I can still taste the upside-down banana splits. We'd sit in the car and exchange toppings or drive along laughing.

Despite all our family time, I didn't feel as if anyone knew me. I don't remember ever talking to anyone about my likes or dislikes. I never shared my feelings about my mom having cancer, or losing a little "sister" to her biological family, or even how it felt to move and go to a different school every year. My family didn't discourage us from expressing ourselves—we regularly had "family meetings" about other things. I wish we would've talked about these too.

I gravitated to church to offset my lack of self-confidence. I logged how many Bible chapters I read or how many verses I memorized—even how long I prayed. I craved perfection. I couldn't mess up. What would people say? After all, I was the preacher's kid and the preacher's grandkid. I just needed to try harder.

But it wasn't enough.

I wasn't enough.

I judged everything I thought, said, or did harshly, getting mad at myself and obsessing over the smallest details. In my teen years, soap operas, romance novels, and pro-feminist teen magazines fascinated me. It was entertainment—my escape.

In college and as a young newlywed, I strained to prove my worth to my professors and classmates, my new family, the world, and God. Most days, I worked from the time I woke up to the time I went to bed. I graduated with my master's, and I had less than a year to finish my PhD. Still, I was empty. I wanted more out of life, but my career was the only thing that gave me worth. If I could just finish the PhD, I would peak. I would be happy—perfect. So, I held on.

After eight years, my husband asked for a divorce. I felt like a hopeless cause. I wanted to be a different person, to make all things right, to measure up. I didn't know how. I studied self-help books. I dabbled in online pornography. Before I knew it, I was addicted. Pornography entangled me. I indulged in unhealthy relationships, suffered broken family relationships, and kept falling behind on the PhD. My body caved under the stress.

I wanted to resign my PhD—to release my grip on being the greatest. Giving up made no sense that far into my education journey, but I did it anyway. Questions echoed through my mind: "Daphne, what will they say?" But the heaviness in my chest released. Within a month-and-a-half, God opened doors to a job and home church in Central Florida.

First Steps to Healing

My new job was the ideal place to start healing. God helped me set boundaries on my workday and resist the urge to sit at the computer a little longer. I couldn't do that on my own. Now? I can turn and walk away—most of the time. Work isn't the solution to my low self-worth. He is.

God then cut the chains of pornography and poor media choices. I stuffed a big black trash bag with everything inappropriate in my house, dragged it to the curb, and took a hammer to it. I didn't even care what the neighbors thought! God, in his miraculous way, took that weight off me. Since then, I've been intentional about what I watch and listen to so I don't fall into that trap.

Despite these significant changes, I was again drawn to unhealthy relationships. I confused dysfunction with love and acceptance, and my health started to suffer again. My doctor recommended counseling. In that first session, I admitted I'm addicted to controlling situations to squash my inner feelings of low self-worth. There's a name for that too! Codependent. I am codependent.

My counselor gave me homework—not the type I'd been accustomed to. I searched for Scriptures about how God truly felt about me. Slowly, I started to believe I matter to God. He loves me for me—not what I do or don't do (Titus 3:4–5). He loved me before I ever did a single thing. He's known me from the beginning (Psalm 139:13). He knows my hurts and struggles; even when I can't express myself, he knows my heart (Romans 8:26). I don't need to perform with God. I can be myself. He won't stop loving me or reject me (Jeremiah 31:3).

Growing Pains

I wanted to help others with their codependent tendencies, so I joined a twelve-step recovery program. I had initial reservations about sharing, much less with women I barely knew. Over time, the hesitation disappeared. With practice, I was able to share without wanting acceptance or a response. My accountability partners didn't hold anything against me, judge me, or treat me differently. I took those tools and set boundaries in relationships—even ended them, if necessary. (Scripts were helpful—both creating and following them.)

Asking for forgiveness for the harm I've done to others is one of the most significant changes in my life. Confessing to others regularly—even saying, "I'm sorry. I was wrong."—has helped me live at peace.

In mid-2009, I was diagnosed as having bipolar depression disorder. I'd seen signs of mental illness in myself, having seen it in family members, but I resisted going to a psychiatrist. Admitting I had a mental illness would be another strike at my self-worth. Looking back, I now understand how my illness has played a part in my overall health and poor decisions. I now accept that it's okay to get help—from family, friends, counselors, doctors, support groups—even medications.

God Keeps Knocking

That same year, I felt restless and disconnected from God. My mind replayed the words of a popular hymn. "Sin had left a crimson stain; He washed me white as snow." An evangelist preached one Sunday about feeling restless when we're not truly saved. All my life, I'd wrestled with that question. I teeter-tottered from "Yep, I'm good" to "I'm not so sure."

Every time, I dismissed it. On that Sunday, I confessed I wasn't sure. I wanted to be certain, to have assurance—and the memory—I'd truly accepted Jesus as my Lord and Savior. Ignoring all the self-criticism—and, *What would they say?*—I took the biggest step in my recovery from codependency. I prayed to receive Jesus with my accountability partner by my side.

God had been drawing me to himself, showing me his love despite my failures and shortcomings. Swallowing my pride—no matter how foolish it might've appeared growing up in church—was my way of showing him. I am white as snow!

Restored

The following year, God revealed my future husband. My Lord chose to give me a second chance and sent me a man who loves me for me. He's seen me with and without meds and still sticks with me. We've endured a lot in ten years: health concerns, job losses, newlywed adjustments, family illnesses, and deaths. My codependent ways surface every now and then, but thanks to God and my recovery tools, I recognize them and reset. My husband has learned some tools too!

The next year, we adopted three siblings. Parenting is teaching me a lot more about codependency. I'm trying not to control or respond in anger, not to rescue my children from bad choices, but communicating in a healthy manner. It's extremely difficult, especially with children of trauma. They, too, have learned some tools.

Two years ago, our family was turned upside-down when a family member brought pornography into our house—the safe space I'd protected for thirteen years. Porn-related activities had been going on for months, unbeknown to us. Our trust was broken, so we installed cameras and ramped up security measures.

I've mourned. I cry for what this person can never undo. I cry for the way it has hurt our family. No one looks at each other the same way. It has suffocated us. I've talked with God about it.

I'm grateful I've accepted Jesus. Otherwise, I would wander helpless and hopeless. God alone has eased my anger and feelings of betrayal. He's giving me opportunities to use the recovery tools I've learned to daily evaluate my attitude and behaviors, to forgive and seek forgiveness, and to restore our home. It's an ongoing process. We're seeing glimmers of hope.

God makes us white as snow. He returns what the Enemy steals. And from bad, he creates good. I made bad choices with relationships. He turned them around to know true love. I grew up with a low self-image. He turned that around so I could help three children who had low self-worth. I grieved a sister when her parents took her back. He turned that around so I could help my children with multiple losses. I moved every year growing up, and he turned that around so I could relate to my children, who'd spent three years in foster homes. Now, he is using my previous struggles with pornography to help a family member overcome theirs. Only God can perform such miracles.

I stumble—my husband and children can attest to that. But God restores—like new, but better. He can do the same for you.

Renew and Restore

- What hurts have had a significant impact on your life?
- Look up Titus 3:4–5 and Jeremiah 31:3. How can these verses help you overcome your hurts and poor choices? Write them out in a journal and express your thoughts.
- Name one specific way you can let God repurpose what you've gone through so it can help someone else. Then, identify where you can connect with someone else who needs your encouragement.

Daphne Tarango comforts others with the comfort she's received from God. Her work has appeared in magazines and anthologies, including *Just Between Us* and *Mentoring Moments for Christian Women*. Daphne has published praise journals, recovery helps, and devotionals for those with mental illnesses. She has co-authored three short story collections. Daphne enjoys solitude, the arts, and spending time with her husband, her three children, their three dogs, and their two cats. Visit Daphne at DaphneWrites.com.

Blooms of Faith

Nancy Graves

*A**ntiques can be expensive, though* every now and then, you may find a piece worth paying up for. But rarer still is the hidden gem forgotten by time, deemed of little value, and tossed aside to lay amid the dust and clutter indefinitely. It was a Saturday afternoon when we found ours.

Relative newlyweds, my husband and I had come to enjoy our weekend excursions to a nearby town where quaint shops and a homemade ice cream parlor sat atop a cobbled hill, just off the beaten path. We went there often to sift through the row of antique stores, taking our time to discover the relics of yesteryear.

It was in one of these shops we had purchased our first set of *real* furniture a few years earlier. And although it was a lot of money for us then, the quality was good, and it would last a lifetime. Energized, we were always on the lookout for another good deal—and our next special purchase. This day, we finally found it. Leaning up against a darkened wall and behind several other pieces, we uncovered a pair of stained-glass panels with delicate pink and yellow tulips set on frosted, crackled glass and framed in old wood. They were beautiful!

After living in a one-bedroom upstairs apartment for our first year of marriage—with a leaky waterbed, hand-me-downs, and a rottweiler—we had saved enough money for the closing costs on an assumable loan mortgage. Although stretched thin, we were very excited to have our own home. And wouldn't you know, the entryway to our little Cape Cod had two perfectly shaped windows on either side of the front door to hang these gorgeous antique stained-glass panels. I was ecstatic! I felt so blessed and thanked God—not only for our new house but for such a precious gift to make it feel like home.

Let the Work Begin!

The realities of homeownership quickly kicked in. The reason we were able to afford our little starter home was that it needed not just a little TLC but a whole lot of tough love.

The kitchen cabinets were from the sixties with missing hardware and chipped paint, and only half of the backsplash tiles remained. The outdated wallpaper was torn. The linoleum was scratched and yellowed. The water heater sat in an opening between the living room and the bathroom, hissing and percolating at will. It was the first thing to greet us each morning and a daily reminder of the tasks that lay ahead.

We didn't have money to pay a contractor to come in with a team of guys to knock out the repairs, so although my husband and I worked hard at our day jobs, we soon came to understand the term *weekend warrior*—which really meant working anytime we were home.

Little by little, the renovations came together. We sided the house in vinyl and painted the trim. We planted bushes and made a flower box. We patched the walls in some rooms and paneled walls in others. We knocked a hole in the ceiling and put in a spiral staircase to gain a loft bedroom. And my husband even built a closet to enclose the water heater—the man had skills. It was the most beautiful closet I had ever seen!

The transformation was slow, but month-by-month and year-by-year, a steady change took shape. But more important than the work being done to the house was the work being done in me. We didn't have much, but I was learning to trust God for our needs, waiting patiently for his provision. And although many of our friends were doing well financially and able to build new houses, for which we were happy for them, I was so grateful for what God had provided for us.

Every time I came home and pulled into the driveway, I would look at my beautiful stained-glass tulips—the first blooms of blessing from the Lord in our lives.

Let the Family Begin!

Life had become very full. Between work and house renovations, church life, and each of our families, the years flew by. We had lived in our house for over five years already, and with it being in much better shape now, we began to think about starting our own family.

I was pushing thirty and had heard the stories of women waiting too long to get pregnant, then not being able to or having difficult pregnancies. Like so many things in life, I thought that only happened to other people. I was healthy, didn't drink or smoke, and exercised regularly. I expected to be pregnant within a month.

That didn't happen.

Somewhat miffed, I resigned myself to repeat the test the following month.

Negative.

Another month went by.

Negative.

After roughly six months, at last I had a positive pregnancy test. I was so excited and quietly relieved. I had not expected it to take that long. But I was finally pregnant, so all was well.

We told our family and all our friends, and everyone rejoiced with us—until the following month when I was rushed to the hospital with bleeding. I had an ectopic pregnancy, not viable and requiring surgery. We had lost our first child.

One of my fallopian tubes needed to be removed, which essentially cut my chances of getting pregnant again in half. More life changes. This time, not so happy.

My doctor put me on medicine to increase my ovulation, which was meant to counter the odds against me. I began to dread taking the pregnancy test. I tried to steel my heart to accept another "failure." But each month, it seemed to hurt more. Time had become my worst enemy.

Although there had been many challenges and severe loss along the path of my life to this point, the thought of never having children left me in a daze. I remembered Hannah from the book of 1 Samuel, how she cried out to the Lord, heartbroken. I now understood her pain.

At the time, I worked in the nursery of my church and with the toddlers. They were so precious, and I loved them. It was a constant reminder of what I may never have. The pain stabbed at my heart.

Now when I came home and parked in my driveway, I'd see our cozy little house and the beautiful blooms from God, but somehow, they seemed cold. Yet, this was still our respite, the shelter from the storms of life that the Lord had provided. I chose to cling to him in the midst of the long, empty days to come.

After an entire year had passed, filled with many tears and much prayer, Bible reading, and talking with others who experienced the same thing, I unexpectedly found myself pregnant. My husband and I were overjoyed!

I had resigned myself to God's will, whatever that would be, but did not give up hope that he may grant me children one day. I was so thankful! Although it took a year, I knew God had a reason. He knew best, and I did not. He had used my pain—once again.

Blooms of Faith

By the time the baby was due to be born, it would be eight years that we had lived in the house. And with the baby coming, we began to realize how small our two-bedroom starter home really was.

We had saved a little money, and after praying about it, we decided to look for a little bit bigger house. We felt it was God's will. And I could hardly believe where the Lord led us. We found a little bigger house not far away—with two perfectly sized cinder block windows in which to hang my beloved stained-glass blooms! This house was clearly God's will for us.

Trouble in Paradise

Our house sold within a month—another confirmation from the Lord. However, after signing all the paperwork and basically sealing the deal, a few days later, I suddenly had a horrific thought. We had not specified in the contract that the stained-glass windows were not part of the deal.

I was grief-stricken—I loved those pieces! I struggled terribly at the thought of leaving them behind and letting them go, not just because of what they had come to mean to me over the years, but because they would fit perfectly in our new house! I wanted them to continue to be a part of our lives, to continue to beautify and cheer us and continue to remind us of God's faithfulness. I lay in bed, fretting and losing sleep.

Taking a hard look at the situation and reflecting on the big picture, I realized I was being unthankful for all the Lord had provided! I had a precious baby on the way—a miracle in itself. We had a beautiful new house, and we had our health and our families. I was so blessed! I prayed and asked God to forgive me. As with all the other struggles, I needed to get to a point where I turned it over to him—accepting whatever he allowed—because he knows best, and he loves me.

Within a few days, we received a call. The real estate agent realized we hadn't specified whether or not we wanted the stained-glass windows. They were still considered our personal property, and we could keep them. The Lord is so gracious!

I learned, whether I had those windows or not, I could trust whatever the Lord allows in my life. He is worth more than any "thing" on earth.

Renew and Restore

- Remember a time when you experienced a trial, but God faithfully met your need. How can this inspire hope for what you're trusting him to do now?

- Have you ever struggled with a desire for material stuff? Make a list of the character qualities of God that are infinitely more valuable than those things you wish for.
- In light of the greater worth of having Jesus Christ instead of any "thing" this world can offer, what material struggle are you ready to surrender to God's will?

Nancy Graves is a freelance writer and editor. She is the author of print and online articles, a blog contributor, and a member of several book launch teams. As an adult student, she served on the staff of her college newspaper, *The Tartan*, eventually stepping into the role of editor in chief. She is the recipient of several ICCJA awards. She writes fiction and non-fiction in various genres. Nancy can be reached at nleegraves@gmail.com.

A Beautiful Mind

Robyn Mulder

I'm not much of a decorator. While some people get rid of entire room sets and purchase something new every few years to keep up with the latest styles, I tend to stick with what I already have.

When I married my husband, I was content with the popcorn ceilings and harvest gold appliances in our house on the farm. The shag carpet didn't bother me too much, and I even stomached the entirely purple bedroom Gary's sister had requested when his family built the house in 1975.

Later, God called my husband from farming to ministry, and we started moving. First, a rental house while he attended two years of college. We didn't have the freedom to do much decorating there. Next, we lived in an old house while he attended three years of seminary. The woodwork and leaded windows were beautiful, but we couldn't do much to make it our own. After seminary, we've lived in three parsonages. All three churches were very generous with the houses they provided, but when you have to get renovations approved by a committee, you tend to live with what you have.

As far as interior decorating goes, our house looks rather sparse, but the things I display on the walls and shelves are familiar and comfortable. They remind me of good times in the past and people we've met over the years.

Mind Decorations

I tend to treat my mind in much the same way. At least, I used to. Certain thoughts "decorated" that space inside my brain. I thought things that were comfortable for years because they were familiar, but they were not beautiful thoughts at all.

I can't.

No one likes me.

I don't know how to do this.

I messed up again.

Why can't I be perfect?

My thoughts constructed a mind with walls of worry and a popcorn ceiling of pessimism. I would try to slap up a few positive thoughts once in a while to cover the insecurities, but they never lasted long. I often had times of distress and depression when those old negative thoughts built up like several layers of ugly wallpaper in an old house.

The Walls Come Down

In 2014, my comfortable mind decorations—and the walls themselves—came tumbling down.

After subbing for several years in our local high school, a full-time position opened up. I applied and was hired to be their Spanish teacher. I was nervous because I hadn't taught full-time for over twenty years, but I was excited about passing on my love of Spanish to the students I'd been getting to know while I subbed.

I spent the summer researching a new method for teaching foreign languages, and then I spent a few days decorating. Colorful posters of Spanish-speaking countries, a bulletin board full of encouraging Spanish expressions, and helpful word lists adorned the walls of my new classroom.

I should have spent some time redecorating the walls of my mind before I started teaching. I had slapped up a few hopeful thoughts like: *I can do this! This is going to be so much fun. I'm going to be the best teacher ever!*

But the realities of teaching a group of typical teenagers soon revealed what I was *really* thinking. I did a good job, but I also made mistakes. My mind replayed them over and over, and I couldn't relax and move on. I wanted every student to love Spanish, and I wanted to teach perfectly. I didn't congratulate myself on the students who had fun in class. Instead, I stressed about the few who walked into class and announced, "I hate Spanish!" The hopeful thoughts disappeared, like the posters losing their grip on the concrete walls of my classroom and ending up on the floor.

My real thoughts took over. *This is hard. I'm not doing this right! They don't like me. I can't do this!* The stress and anxiety continued to rise. I couldn't sleep at night. I had a constant ache in my stomach, and I could hardly eat. I held it together and hid my feelings pretty well in front of my students, but at home, I would cry as I stared at my blank lesson plan book. The anxiety paralyzed me, and I could hardly stay ahead of each day's preparations.

When Hope Is Gone

After just a month of this, my hope was gone. I had seen a doctor and started taking a couple of medications, but they weren't working fast enough, and my brain chemistry continued to deteriorate. I would try to think good thoughts, and I listened to encouraging songs on the way to school, but I reached a point where the depression was clinical, and I could no longer help myself.

I went to the basement one day and wrapped an extension cord around my neck in my hopelessness. Thankfully, I came to my senses before I went any further. I threw the cord down and went back upstairs. Telling my husband how I felt added even more reality to the situation, and we made plans to go to the hospital the next day. Of course, we couldn't go immediately because I had work to do. I wanted to die, but I still felt responsible for getting my midterm grades figured out. The thoughts inside my head didn't make any sense at all. It was time for some major repairs.

Learning to Redecorate

I spent almost a week in the mental health unit of our regional hospital. It was there that I finally started learning to redecorate the walls of my mind. In group sessions, I learned about how important our thoughts are when it comes to mental health. When I felt better, I started to journal about what I was feeling and thinking. So much of it was distorted thinking that affected how I interacted with others and kept me from enjoying the life God had given me.

After I got home, I saw a counselor and continued the difficult process of tearing down many of my old thoughts and renovating my mind. I used Philippians 4:8 as I decided what could stay and what had to go: "Fix your thoughts on what is true, and honorable, and right, and pure, and lovely, and admirable. Think about things that are excellent and worthy of praise."

It's still more familiar and comfortable to slap up the old ways of thinking, but I'm getting better at recognizing those ugly old thought posters that cover up what's excellent and praiseworthy. What's even better is the fact that when I fix my thoughts on all of those good things, they stay put. They become part of the beautiful permanent design of my brain, not just temporary artwork that might blow down when stressful situations arise.

I'm thankful for that major depressive episode. Hard as it was, it got me to better places emotionally. I was limping along through life, settling for the trash talk Satan threw at me and the lies I had chosen to believe about myself. Getting that sick forced me to examine how I was thinking. I see it as a precious treasure from God when I look back at the love people showed me during that time and the things God showed me about myself.

Constant Renovations

It's fine for me to live in a house with artwork and pictures that have followed us through multiple ministry moves. Those things are beautiful and timeless. But I can't move through life with the same old thoughts in my mind. Some of them were beautiful and useful for a while, but the Holy Spirit gently points out the ones that have to go because they're outdated or because they were lies I had believed all along. He'll help me rip down the layers of ugly ideas and thoughts, like those layers of old wallpaper, and together we can redecorate with the truth.

If I catch the lying thoughts as soon as possible, they'll never even make it onto the walls of my mind. I can enjoy a godly sense of style in my thought life, and I'll never have to go back to those depressing times again.

It's going to be exciting to see what God does with the place.

Renew and Restore

- Take a look around your mind. What thoughts decorate the walls in there? Set a timer for five minutes and write down what you're thinking.
- Now read over your list. Are those thoughts positive and beautiful? Or are they negative and ugly?
- Cross out any thoughts you want to tear down. Write down thoughts to replace them that will beautify your brain and get you to healthier emotional places.

Robyn Mulder grew up in Michigan but married a good-looking farmer in Iowa after college. She went on to live in Michigan, Minnesota, Iowa, and now South Dakota after her husband felt his call into ministry. She and Gary have four adult children. Robyn is an editor and writer who also loves to turn scrap pieces of paper into works of art in her craft room. www.robynmulder.com

Loss and God's Goodness

Ruth Black

It was my third pregnancy loss. Twice within our first year of marriage, my husband and I experienced this sorrow. It was heartbreaking. But we recovered as best we could.

Finally, after almost a year of trying, I conceived again. We were so thrilled. We got in to see the OB doctor very early, and I was closely monitored. All seemed fine. We got to see our little unborn baby's heart beating fast at just five and a half weeks on December 22. That was a joy we had not experienced with our other pregnancies, which both ended before a heartbeat was detected. Though I struggled with nausea and fatigue, I rejoiced at these symptoms of what I hoped was a healthy pregnancy.

The New Year began with high hopes and dreams of our future baby. On January 12, I had another ultrasound. I was about eight and a half weeks along. The technician was too quiet. I am not an expert on reading ultrasounds, but I sensed something was wrong. She measured the fetus, my baby. She checked again. Finally, in a quiet, tense voice, she spoke. "I'm not getting a heartbeat."

She left the room to inform the nurse practitioner on duty. I slid off the table and turned to my husband. It was a moment of indescribable shock and pain. Somehow, the tears stayed at bay in the next several minutes. We met with the nurse practitioner, who told us our options. We could wait and let nature take its course or have a procedure called a D&C to remove the fetal tissue and placenta from my womb. Still in shock, I opted to wait at that point. We left. I broke down in the elevator. I sobbed as we walked past people in the hallway. I couldn't stop the flood of tears.

I don't remember much about the next few days. A blur of tears, fears, and decisions. We went back on Friday for another ultrasound. I had to be sure. I couldn't live with myself if I was wrong. But we weren't. There was no sign of life. And so, I decided to have a D&C the following Wednesday.

I was relieved to get it over with that Wednesday morning. But I was also nervous as I kissed Matt goodbye as they wheeled me to the OR.

Experiencing God's Goodness Through Others

The next thing I knew, I was awake. The hospital staff was so kind. I was cared for so well. A bit woozy from pain meds, I felt no emotional or physical pain as I waited in a recovery room for a few hours, sipping on Sprite or dozing off. Finally, the kind nurse helped me walk to the side entrance where Matt was waiting with the car. She wrapped a warm blanket around me and gently praised my good husband as I shuffled to the door. I agreed with her assessment. "Yes, he treats me so well," I said. She insisted I keep the blanket.

I spent the next couple of days recovering physically. I did nothing but watch Netflix, eat, and sleep. Friends brought food, sent cards, and texted me. My mom came over and just sat with me for hours. My brothers dropped off a brownie mix. (They know me well!) I tried to go out on Saturday for the first time since the surgery. I was exhausted after just a trip to the gas station. So, we went back home.

Experiencing God's Goodness Through His Word

Although I woke up feeling better on Sunday morning, I chose to stay home from church. My darling husband got ready to go preach, and I told him I'd be praying for him. I stayed in bed almost the entire morning watching *The Bible* miniseries on Netflix. In the next few hours, I experienced a quiet but strong sense of God's presence comforting me through the familiar stories that I saw dramatized on my television. As the suffering of Sarah played on the screen, I felt her pain and understood her desire to give her husband a child at any cost, only to experience the bitter jealousy that accompanied her unwise plot. Then, later, I saw the agony of God's people in Egypt under the cruelty of Pharaoh, seemingly forgotten by their God. I understood what it was to feel forsaken and unloved. I wondered again for the thousandth time why God chose to hide his face for so long at times (in their case, hundreds of years).

A comforting thought slowly formed in my mind that Sunday morning. Suffering knows no boundaries. It touches everyone—even followers of God. God permits it, although it was not part of his original design.

God creates life. He had placed our unborn children within the womb. But did he also cause them to die? I couldn't reconcile that thought with what I know about God. I believe God is sovereign. And so, I believe he allows and uses even the worst evil for his purposes and for the good of his children. But I do not believe he causes evil. When we saw no heartbeat, God was not the one causing that death. He was the One sustaining us in that painful moment and in all the painful moments to come. He is the giver of life, the creator of blessings, the one who fills a barren woman's home with the laughter of children.

I was a grieving woman, but not without hope. Matthew 5:4 says, "God blesses those who mourn, for they will be comforted." I chose to believe that even if I never cradled a child in my arms, God was for me. I trusted in this good God. Though I struggled to pray at first and could barely comprehend that God loved me, I know he never left my side. His heart was filled with compassion. I don't understand why he didn't intervene and keep my baby alive. But I do know that he holds my baby—all three of my babies—in his loving arms.

Experiencing God's Goodness through His Good Gifts

When autumn rolled around that year, I discovered I was pregnant again. The following spring, a healthy baby boy was placed in my arms. He is now a rambunctious bundle of three-year-old energy with big blue eyes and a mischievous smile. Not a day goes by that I don't hug him and feel my heart beating outside of my body and whisper, "Thank you, God, for this gift." I still don't know why we walked through the valley of sorrow. But I know the Giver of Life. And he says, "Weeping may last through the night, but joy comes with the morning" (Psalm 30:5).

Perhaps you've walked through valleys such as this. In the midst of these seasons, it can feel as though God is a million miles away. Leaning into the big picture of God's work in the world is so helpful. Allowing the eternal truths of the gospel to invade your soul can begin a healing process unlike anything else. He is with us, even in the middle of the valley. Trust him. His ways are good.

Renew and Restore

- When have you trusted God in the midst of heartbreak? What was the most difficult part of your experience? What was the most encouraging?
- What Bible verses have sustained you in the middle of seasons of sadness? Write several out on cards to keep with you or to give to others who need encouragement.
- How has God shown you his character in unexpected ways, even when you felt confused or angry?

Ruth Black is a wife to Matt and a mom to James. Together, they live in the mountains of Eastern Kentucky, where her husband is on staff at a Bible college. Ruth desires to help women see the beauty of the gospel in everyday life. She writes for a variety of Christian publications. She also enjoys writing her thoughts at her blog: littlemoments-bigdreams.blogspot.com.

Beneath the Layers

Amy Marcoux

Strong knowing hands poise above me. I inhale and become aware of the mingled aroma of raw pine and varnish. I think I might be able to reach out and catch the late afternoon rays of sun floating on the sawdust that hangs in the workshop air. My eyes flutter closed as weathered hands come near. I tense as a strong metal tool meets my vulnerable exterior. In one stroke, decades of layers peel into a spiral beneath its cold blade.

I hold my breath and brace for the next scrape. Shivering, I cringe, considering what these hands will discover under my careful design. It has been so meticulously covered for so long. Not even I know what original substance lies beneath.

How quickly my story runs ahead of itself. I am sure there was a time when my grain shone proudly. My Maker enthusiastically added his stamp and ran his finger along the smooth finish. He must have smiled. I was new, fresh, and so full of promise. Every masterpiece the table-maker crafts is designed with intent. He knew my purpose and could not wait for me to discover it.

Just Enough to Please

I am that piece crafted by loving hands. My years of living so much like its layered surface. My childhood home was warm and happy. Many people came through our door for meals, support, conversation, and friendship.

We cleaned and polished a lot before they came. We loved deeply and liked to accommodate. Others' thoughts were important to us. This cultivated an unquenchable desire for approval in my young heart alongside the strong will etched in my soul. It did not take me long to realize that I could behave, speak, present, and design myself in such a way that would be sure to catch an eye.

And so, I began to paint. A sweet, agreeable, childlike veneer. Brushed just along my grain. Just enough tint to please.

Sunrise and sunset gave rhythm to the days, months, and years. Time brought many relationships and interactions that taught me to navigate expectations. I frequently pushed myself to assume burdens that exceeded my capacity. As long as I can remember, I was able to look into someone's eyes and know how they felt. I knew how to be what they wanted.

Much to my enthusiasm, I discovered that when I took on extra responsibility, I'd receive trust, control, opportunity, and identity in return. Those with noble intentions praised me as I performed and rarely missed a chance to remind me that I was loved by God. Somehow, this made me paint even more. If he loved me, it must be my job to please him, too.

I made it my purpose to design, to achieve, to win. I positioned myself to look just right. If I wanted someone to like me, I made sure they did. If I was supposed to be a good girl, I was. I followed the rules. I worked and studied hard. I planned for everything. I graduated at the top of my class and attended college on a full-tuition scholarship. I managed a retail shop at eighteen years of age and bought a house before twenty.

Life was vibrant, satisfying, and full of interesting people. I fell madly in love with one of those people and married a man as layered and motivated as myself. He had been designed with great empathy, cultivated to make an impression, and was well accustomed to carrying the burdens of others. Our powers combined, and adult life began.

Together, We Painted

We painted boldly. We added stripes where most wouldn't dare add stripes. We liked it when people noticed us. We were excited when our pattern inspired others. It was clear from the beginning that we were better together. Side by side, we felt there was nothing we could dream that we couldn't do. Dreams, challenges, and accomplishments kept us energized and reaching for the next thing.

We followed our passions to love, please, and care for people right into a life of ministry. Never had we felt more vibrant. Serving our community, contributing to exciting change, and always facing a new challenge invigorated us. We led ministries, ran programs, and raised children. We navigated finances, family dynamics, and business meetings. I smiled and posed. Sometimes my legs felt tired from so much holding and supporting.

Some people were messy, and they were not always careful with me. Like thoughtless users who mar an heirloom piece, the words and actions of some left gouges and dings on my soul. Others brought me their tears from broken hearts. They let them pool on my surface and soak into the fiber of my being. Water stains darkened my exterior. I grasped for control to steady myself and clung to the identity I nurtured. I needed people to need me, and subconsciously, I vowed I would never need them back.

Hairline Cracks

It made sense to me that if I could keep my fragility under the surface, I could help others with theirs. It felt noble to cover up. It positioned me to help, to listen, to care. It kept me from burdening someone else. Years passed, and like hairline cracks that begin to sprawl through treasured pieces, exhaustion crept through my being. My strength, confidence, and drive began to falter, but I refused to let anyone see my shame.

I quietly worked to cover my vulnerable places in the dark. I'd layer on a smile in hopes of concealing the imperfections that kept bleeding through. I just needed to look worthy. All the hiding gave me an impression of control but left me lost and grasping again at the end of each day. I began to feel bitter about the weight I was holding. It seemed easier to push people away than to invite them into my struggle. In a strange twist of plot, I pridefully showed everyone I was ok and resented them for believing me.

Resentment spread and turned me brittle. A new workplace full of well-meaning others with similar tendencies produced an environment of disapproval, blame, and duplicity. The very mission we depended on to unite us had the capacity to break us as we insisted on proving our sufficiency. An unexpected betrayal from trusted leadership flooded my life with doubt.

The ground shifted, and the dovetails loosened. I staggered and nearly fell apart in the disappointment and fear of how my reputation and family would be impacted. People that mattered to me confirmed my fears that it would be easier to discard us than to stand with us. Soon after the disruption, our whole life changed. It was time to move, and I did not withstand change well.

Always and Never

A physical injury during our move surprised my usual resilience, and frayed nerves refused to allow healing. A startling diagnosis ushered in devastating news. My legs could no longer hold even my own weight. Chronic edicts of "always" and "never" splashed carelessly across the veneer I'd cultivated. Pain was my constant companion. Years of exceeding my capacity had tilted the equilibrium of my nervous system, and the injury tipped the balance.

The prognosis of neurological damage threatened to progressively spread excruciating pain throughout my limbs before turning its attention to my vital organs. My weakness was exposed. In my agony, I could not even raise my brush.

The darkness brought questions I dared not admit in the morning light. How much longer would I have to endure? What would become of all I had tried to create? What purpose could this pile of broken dreams serve? My compassionate husband held my hands tightly and begged me to look into his eyes as he tried to fill me with words of hope. He and my children and many others reminded me that I was loved and valuable. I struggled to believe them. How could I be loved if I had nothing to offer?

My every need was now something for someone else to carry. What once seemed so shiny suddenly appeared dull and useless.

In my despair, when I could no longer lift my hands, I felt the Maker's hands lift my broken pieces. A hint of recognition in the gentle finger running over rough, damaged edges. A faded stamp in a hidden place confirmed what those hands already knew. The One who created me could see what remained in the deterioration. He knew his hands could yet reveal the beauty I lived to cover.

Beneath the Layers

Dearest reader, you bear the stamp too. In the hidden place, that reminder that you were created with intent. I don't know what makes your legs weak right now. Maybe you are still hiding. Perhaps no one has yet noticed the way you wobble under the weight of each day. Maybe you have been discarded and have already lost hope. If you have breath, there is more for you. Close your eyes. Inhale and surrender to those knowing hands. He is waiting to reveal the value hiding beneath your layers—the beauty of the natural grain and texture.

I realize I have been holding my breath. With my long-awaited exhale, there comes a new lightness. A second opinion told me of a nontraditional treatment. It held no promises, and it meant leaving my family for months, but I knew I had to try. After months of treatments, neurological restructuring, and relentless physical therapy, I achieved remission from a disease that does not often give up its grasp. Those months stripped me to my core. The stripping has left me raw, but a natural glow is returning to the surface as I learn to depend on my Maker's strong hands.

Restoration has been costly and time-consuming, but his unhurried grasp tells me I am worth it. Reassembly requires daily trust and surrender of the weight for which I thought I was responsible. I will never be the same, and I still do not understand each new adjustment. I am getting used to my new measurements.

Steady hands spend extra time working on tender places where others have not been so gentle. He's kindly showing me that each ring of the rich grain we've discovered under the layers tells not only my own but the many stories that have impacted mine. Without the layers, the stories can glow.

The dust is still settling. A protective finish will take patient time to cure.

I have a glimpse of my new view. He has placed me on display in the space he imagined. I'm being filled with his treasures, and I have a front-row view of his daily work. I am loved. He invites people to run their finger over the scars my pain has carved. This deep texture causes each one to take pause and appreciate the restorative work of the artist. His work has incorporated me into his story, and he will not allow more than my legs can bear. The last rays of sun linger at the window, and I realize he has positioned me to catch their reflection. I shine. A table for his glory.

Renew and Restore

- What is hiding under your carefully manicured layers?
- What are the places in your life where knowing hands need to repair wounds from where others have not been so gentle?
- As you surrender to the hands that can repurpose your life, the process might be difficult. What fear keeps you from full surrender to God's work on your layers?

Amy Marcoux is an energetic adventure-seeking writer, mentor, wife, and mother of three girls in a home full of personality. She is a strong-willed perfectionist who tries to do it all and wants people to think she has it all together. She is learning, through the unexpected, to let go and to share her real life so that she can point others to the hope she has found. You can find her blog at goletgo.org.

Surprised By Doubt

Sue Donaldson

In my early twenties and in my second year at a small Christian college, I woke up one day and was surprised to realize I had lost my faith. In a quiet panic, I wondered to myself, *Is Christianity really true? Have I been duped? Does God even exist? Were my parents mistaken?*

Immersed in great Bible classes, surrounded by godly professors and Christian friends, and attending chapel five days a week, I couldn't understand from where these unbidden and frightening thoughts came.

Certainly not from anything I could figure out. No one spoke about doubts. Chapel speakers, pastors, and professors never broached the subject.

The fact remained: I had lost my faith, and I felt as if I was living on the edge of crazy. Sick and worried and worried-sick, I kept these questions to myself. Giving voice to my doubts gave credence. I didn't want to give them credence.

Only God

Several months into my doubts, I hashed it out with a God I wasn't sure existed. Traveling through the mountains in the state of Washington, I discovered a sky full of stars. They were hard to miss. I hailed from Los Angeles, where there were stars of the Hollywood variety but not many above that could be seen with the naked eye.

Finally, gratefully, surrounded by a dark sky, spangled and sequined, I concluded: *God must have created all this. There is too much beauty around me to reject a Creator's existence.*

My cautious first step back to faith was rooted in the Bible in the book of Romans: "They know the truth about God because he has made it obvious to them. For ever since the world was created, people have seen the earth and sky. Through everything God made, they can clearly see his invisible qualities—his eternal power and divine nature. So they have no excuse for not knowing God" (Romans 1:19–20).

God tells us we can know him, and he begins with what he does best: making stuff. We know someone in part by what they make and how they make it. And what God made was great.

That week in the mountains made me sit up and take notice. Only God could go to such detail. Only God could set up the turning of the planets, the schedule of the seasons, the effect of a bee's nose in a dahlia.

God invited me to examine what he had made, and it made sense to me that, at the least, he was Creator God.

It was a start.

Only God would go to the trouble of declaring and proclaiming to a twenty-something alone on a mountain. I needed proof to believe again, and the stars were calling my name. I only needed to open my eyes.

God doesn't call you and me to a blind faith, but when we live with one eye closed, we curry unnecessary doubt. Recognizing God's handiwork helped me begin my step back to faith, and I began to pray, "Lord, give me eyes to see what you have made. Remove the blinders. Help me pay attention to your grandeur and beauty. Thank you, and amen."

Someone To Be Weak With

Sometime later, I took a late-night walk with Mrs. Dunkin. I didn't know her well. *Not well enough*, I thought, *to share my dark secret of doubt*. But she seemed safe. I knew she was gentle and unassuming, and again, it was dark. A light shines brighter in the dark, and I was desperate for light.

I wanted to share my anxious thoughts with her, but I hesitated with that closed-throat feeling when you are sure you are going to cry and you'd rather not blubber in public, even when it's only one person, even when you know most people don't care if you do. In the end, I choked out my confession.

"Mrs. Dunkin," I whispered, "I have doubts."

Unruffled and unperturbed, she replied with magical words. I call them *magical* because I had never heard them before, and God used them to work magic on my bruised and worried soul.

"Oh, Sue, everyone doubts."

Everyone doubts? News to me. No one I knew ever spoke of doubts. Another surprise. This time, a welcomed one. Such words of comfort and relief.

I felt alone in my doubts. But sharing with someone older and wiser steadied my uncertain steps. Mrs. Dunkin told me that doubts are common. Just hearing that simple truth began to break through my fear. Though I felt on the edge of crazy, I wasn't crazy altogether nor all by myself. *Everyone doubts.*

I would not have heard her words if I had not shared my own. Singular vulnerability can be terrifying, but it's worth the risk when sharing your story with someone older who has lived life and come out the other side—wiser, calmer, and sitting in a place of love rather than judgment.

We all need someone we can be weak with, someone with whom we can express our doubts. Someone who can hold out a lifeline of truth from God's Word and a story of how he worked those truths into their one true life.

God doesn't call you and me to a solitary faith, doing life all by ourselves.

I continue to pray, "Lord, God, thank you for someone to be weak with in my time of need. May I be the one to come alongside another and let her know she is not alone. To tell her that no matter what, you can be trusted. Thank you, and amen."

God is Big Enough

In the fall of that year, God met me again with simple truth. Doubts persisted, which made me wonder if they might never end. I hesitantly broached the subject with my favorite professor. I remember exactly where we stood on the sidewalk between Vyder and Rutherford Hall when a brief but poignant exchange made all the difference. "Mr. Hills," I began, not wanting to cry, especially now in front of a teacher I respected and loved.

"Mr. Hills," I said again, "I have doubts."

As I think back now, I wonder how he grasped the gravity of that statement. I didn't explain nor elaborate. I couldn't trust my voice. Yet somehow, his words hit the mark. He looked off into who knows where— one never quite knew with favorite English professors where their heads might be. All I know is he didn't look at me until he replied gently, yet matter-of-factly, "Well, Sue, if God couldn't handle our questions, he wouldn't be a big enough God, would he?" He chuckled mildly, and we kept walking.

That was it. I don't think there was anything else. I may have nodded, and we went on our way, no more discussion. But it was enough. God was big enough or he wasn't God. Big enough to handle anything I might throw his way: questions, doubts, anger, even accusations.

Even people in the Bible struggled with their doubts and fear. King David cried out in anguish: "'O God my rock,' I cry, 'Why have you forgotten me?'" (Psalm 42:9). "How long will you look the other way?" (Psalm 13:1).

Many more biblical figures such as Abraham, Job, and Moses, and a host of others second-guessed what they heard, defended their doubts, even laughed. But God didn't run from them, nor push them away. Nor will he run from you and me.

Perhaps what God wanted me to learn most during my drought of faith was not the answers to my questions, but rather an answer to his question: "How big do you think I am, Sue?" Once that question was settled, all others could wait to be answered.

God doesn't call you and me to a cowering faith, and he's not intimidated by our skepticism nor rattled when we are rattled. He loves us too much to be insulted when we approach him with humble and desperate questions.

I pray gratefully, "Lord, God, thank you that you don't shy away from my doubts, nor give up on my dubious faith. Grant me a deeper conviction of your greatness, a wider appreciation of your love. Thank you, and amen."

He Wants Us to Want Him

Around that time, I read a familiar verse as if for the first time. "So faith comes from hearing, that is, hearing the Good News about Christ" (Romans 10:17). There it was in black and white. Faith comes from God's Word. Not understanding exactly what that meant, I simply began to read the Bible. Not that I hadn't before, but I was on a mission. I wanted to believe. God was drawing me back to himself.

God is a wooing God. He invites, he doesn't force us. He wants us to want him and then do something about that want: go after him with all you've got.

Jeremiah 29:13 states: "If you look for me wholeheartedly, you will find me."

Over a period of months of reading, praying, seeking, and wanting, my faith gradually returned. God met me in my unbelief and carried me back home. Faith to doubt, then faith restored.

Why this detour in my faith? As comforting as Mrs. Dunkin's words were, now I know that not everyone doubts. Perhaps I needed to figure out how serious I was in my pursuit of God. Perhaps God wanted me to have a faith of my own. I needed to believe for myself, not only because of how I was raised.

As I continue on this road to a deeper, stronger faith, I'm comforted by the candor of a father's desperate cry to Jesus for his son's healing. "I do believe, but help me overcome my unbelief!" (Mark 9:24).

God doesn't call you and me to a perfect faith. My prayer continues to be: "Lord, I'm only this far along in my faith, please make up for the rest. I believe. Help me overcome my unbelief. Thank you, and amen."

Renew and Restore

You may not doubt, but if you do, remember that God is never surprised. Three things may help you continue to seek the Lord with all your heart.

- **Go outside.** If you wonder, "Is this really true?" go outside and tell God you cannot deny what he has made. We are surrounded by evidence.
- **Find a mentor.** Take a walk with someone who will remind you that God was big enough for them and that he will be for you.
- **Come to Jesus.** Tell God you believe, and ask, would he please make up for what you may not yet believe? He may reply to that prayer with his own question: "How much do you want me? Read my Word. Love me and others. And your faith will be what it needs to be."

Sue Donaldson and her husband, Mark, live in San Luis Obispo, California. They've raised three daughters who keep them at the bank and on their knees. Sue loves connecting people to one another, to God, and his Word, and has been speaking for over twenty years. An author of four books, Sue blogs at *Welcome Heart: Knowing and Showing the Heart of God* and hosts a weekly podcast, *Make it Count: Living a Legacy Life.*

Joy in the Messiness of Life

Meaghan Jackson

I *couldn't take it anymore. The* whining and fighting from my children made me feel like a terrible mom. That would just set me off to yell at my kids to stop. It was a vicious cycle, and I didn't know how to make it stop. What made matters worse was that our family business was struggling, and I was worried about finances. At the same time, I had just suffered a second miscarriage and was overcome by grief.

Unfortunately, there is no pause button in life to allow you to catch up—or heal. You must do all these things while life rushes on around you. At the time, I felt numb, guilty, and alone. The neighbors were complaining about the kids, and my family pointed out the effects it was having on my children and me. I couldn't hide our troubles anymore. I had nothing left to give. I was at the end of myself.

Pour Out Your Heart

When I was at my lowest point, I was filled with such grief and anguish that no words could describe what I felt. After my miscarriages, major financial struggles, and family crises, I wanted to cry out to God. I wanted desperately to connect with him, but I couldn't find the words. During those times in my life, I felt God's loving presence around me.

How could he have known what I needed? The Holy Spirit was speaking to my heavenly Father on my behalf. He was interpreting the crying, groaning, deep, and desperate longing in my heart.

> And the Holy Spirit helps us in our weakness. For example, we don't know what God wants us to pray for. But the Holy Spirit prays for us with groanings that cannot be expressed in words. And the Father who knows all hearts knows what the Spirit is saying, for the Spirit pleads for us believers in harmony with God's own will. (Romans 8:26–27)

Your prayers do not have to be perfect and well worded. Throughout the Bible, we hear stories of God hearing the prayers of those whose hearts were in the right place. God wants the imperfect, raw, and honest you. He wants a true relationship where you feel safe to share your anger, frustration, worries, and doubts. And on those days when you just don't even know what to pray, know that the Spirit is there talking to God for you.

The Truth About Who You Are

I am so blessed that he answered my prayers. Several friends offered words of encouragement. They saw my heart and the real me. Their words cut through my brokenness and helped me to see that I had worth and value too. I began to journal and write down notes for myself. I treasured these kind words. Referring to them often when I felt upset, I know God was healing me from the inside out.

So often, we believe the lies that we are not good enough, smart, or pretty enough. These can come from the outside, but more often than not, it is what we tell ourselves. You are more than just a mom, or wife, or sister, or employee. Not only do you have your earthly parents, but you have a loving heavenly Father who cares deeply for you. You are a daughter of the King! You, yes you, the one reading this. You are a princess and heir with Jesus Christ. Can you feel the power and overwhelming love wrapped up in those statements?

The Road to Transformation

When I was struggling, after much prayer and consideration, I knew something needed to change for our family. Swallowing my pride, I finally reached out for help. I took several parenting courses online and in-person. They were very helpful, and I learned a lot of great parenting strategies. I also began to feel more confident as a mom. One thing I know is that most of parenting has to do with the parent. It's what we bring to the relationship that matters.

By working on myself first, I would be bringing healing to the whole family. Not only would I be modeling how healthy adults care for themselves and work through difficult times, but I could directly implement the helpful parenting strategies with my children.

The main parenting strategies I learned all focused on self-regulation and working on myself, connecting with my children, emotion coaching and helping them with their feelings, and simplifying our lives to calm the chaos. By taking baby steps in each of these areas, over time, we saw big changes in how we related to each other while increasing peace in our home.

You are Not Alone

One thing I did notice in all the parenting courses I took was that something was missing. At first, I couldn't put my finger on it, until I realized that God was missing. There are many wonderful parenting courses and parenting books, but so few came with a gentle, peaceful Christian mindset. It was incredibly important for my husband and me that our parenting aligned with any books or courses we used.

We seek to be gentle, peaceful parents. Not permissive or authoritarian but demonstrating the fruit of the spirit in our family. "But the Holy Spirit produces this kind of fruit in our lives: love, joy, peace, patience, kindness, goodness, faithfulness, gentleness, and self-control. There is no law against these things!" (Galatians 5:22–23). These are important character qualities we wanted to model and teach to our children.

I was wary of looking into anything labeled Christian because I wasn't sure if I'd agree with the parenting style. There aren't that many resources available for gentle, peaceful Christian parents. So, I began to heal and transform myself with God's help. Each time I worked through a portion of a course I was taking, I went to God to see that it aligned with his Word. Of course, the Bible consistently points to loving and caring for each other with gentleness and patience.

What I noticed most was that many of the parenting resources I found called for inner strength and pointed at the individual as the one who could make the changes and transformation. But I knew I needed God. With his help, I could do anything. With his strength, I could overcome my weaknesses. It was comforting to know I was not alone. The transforming work of the Holy Spirit was alive and working in my family.

There are many times in life when we do not know where to turn, what to do next, or how to handle a situation. The weight of life and responsibility seems crushing at times. God does not grow weary. He is not burdened by our struggles. He wants us to come to him and share our troubles with him.

When you pour out your troubles and lay them at his feet, our loving heavenly Father will fill you with indescribable peace. "Don't worry about anything; instead, pray about everything. Tell God what you need, and thank him for all he has done. Then you will experience God's peace, which exceeds anything we can understand. His peace will guard your hearts and minds as you live in Christ Jesus" (Philippians 4:6–7).

You may have to wait for your circumstances to change, but you do not need to wait before trusting God to help you through whatever you are facing. You can choose to put your faith in the one who loves you, who made the earth, who can see everything going on behind the scenes.

Even if you don't feel as if you have the strength to continue on or that you have nothing left to give, you don't have to do it all. Once I prayed and gave my problems to the Lord, the weight was lifted. I still had to go through those difficult times. But I now had peace and hope that I would be able to come through it stronger.

On the Other Side of The Struggle

We are a different family now. Through our trials, we have become even better than before because our heavenly Father lovingly brought a change in my husband's heart and mine. I've learned that our trials develop character, endurance, and strength. We are continually growing and changing. Once we know better, we can do better.

We aren't meant to carry the burden, shame, guilt, and power to change all on our own. What a blessing and joy it is that God comes alongside us to help us through. We can ask him for help and rely on his strength when we are weak. I know I would not be where I am today without Christ's power in me. With his help, my family has been transformed. There is more joy, peace, and hope in our home.

Because of this incredible transformation, God placed it on my heart to offer other moms the support I wish I had when I needed it most. He used the hard times in my life to work on my character and give me a passion for serving others. I've taken all the strategies and information I've learned through my training as a parenting coach, placing God's Word at the center, to mentor and support parents. I'm continually learning and growing through helping other mothers.

Now my life is all about joy. I'm not talking about feeling happy, or successful, or anything like that. Those feelings come and go. Life is all about ups and downs. Joy, on the other hand, is intentional. It is about finding something good, some flicker of hope, in all that life brings you.

Right now, my life is busy, to say the least. It is all about raising three boys, homeschooling, running my businesses, and all the while trying not to lose "me" in the midst of it all. My faith keeps me going. I have a God who has been through it all, who loves me so much, and understands how much I need him.

I choose to daily find joy in the life that I have right at this moment.

Live a life of joy. Don't let anything hold you back. Find the good blessings that this day has to offer.

Renew and Restore

- Pour out your heart to God. Share with him all your worries and problems. Ask him now for peace.
- Write down your limiting beliefs and what you tell yourself about who you are. Next, on a new page, write about the new you. Write down the truth and where you are heading. You are a new creation destined for great things.
- Reflect on a time that was a struggle in your life and how God used that time to change you, teach you something, or use you to bless others.
- Make a list of all the blessings, large and small, in your life. Thank God for all these gifts with a joyful heart.

Meaghan Jackson of *Joyful Mud Puddles* is a gentle Christian parenting coach. She has taken her passion for bringing peaceful calm to family life and pairs that with her background in education to help parents become more confident and well equipped. What better way to describe the messy, fun, and exciting life of a mom with three boys than joyful mud puddles! www.joyfulmudpuddles.com

Some Dreams Need to Die

Jodie Cooper

I still remember the day he was born. I remember sitting on the bed, in the dark of the hospital room, cradling this precious new life. I also remember a sudden rush of fear coming over me, cutting through the peacefulness of his newborn sleep. I felt terrified at the thought of high school. Would the other kids be kind to him? Would he make friends? And girlfriends.

It wasn't so easy to shake these feelings of anxiety in the darkness that night, but the following days were filled with joy, celebration, and hope for the future. Those worries seemed far gone.

Over a year later, they resurfaced. Our son seemed happy and healthy, but he didn't communicate much. Just as we began considering seeing a specialist, we started to hear his beautiful little voice. Then came the explosion of animal sounds, words, sentences, and songs. It seemed our fears had been misplaced. He loved to talk.

But the more he grew, and the more I spent time with other mums, I started to notice differences. Every child is different. But he seemed a different kind of different.

There were lots of tears, especially when we were visiting someone or in a group with other families. He didn't have much desire to move, explore, and engage with new environments. Granted, there was a lot of talking going on, but much of it was songs or stories that he knew by heart that he repeated and repeated.

Initially, we thought this was cute. We marveled at his incredible memory and showed off his oral skills with recitations of poems and stories for our guests.

The Diagnosis

At Christmas, we visited my sister and her daughter, who was one year younger than our son. She blew me away. I commented to my sister, "Wow! How did you teach her to be so social?"

She turned and gave me a funny look. "I didn't have to teach her anything," she slowly replied.

This conversation haunted me for the rest of our visit. It caused me to start more conversations, and these led to visits to doctors, pediatricians, and specialists. We were seeking a diagnosis. At no point in that journey did I feel sad or scared. I was hopeful. Hopeful that we would finally get some answers.

After the assessment, a psychologist delivered us the news. "Your son is on the Autism Spectrum."

I felt such relief. Getting to this point had been expensive and stressful, and I was so happy to have the outcome we had expected.

"So, you'll be able to fix him, right?" I responded when asked if we had any questions.

There was a moment's hesitation.

"Look, it's great that you've come to us this early. Early intervention is so important. I can't make any guarantees of how he will respond to therapy and . . ."

I don't remember any more of her words. My head was spinning. As much as I'd thought he did have ASD, I had been excited to get the diagnosis, to start getting therapy and help because I naively thought that if we knew what it was, we could make it go away.

Dead Dreams

I'd always had hopes and dreams for my son. In my mind, it was just guaranteed that I would raise kids who were socially confident, comfortable, and considerate of others. This rated highly in the "success" stakes for me. But the reality was that my son would often scream at people who spoke to him. I was crippled by the sinking feeling that he might never be as I had imagined.

Over months of reflection and processing, I started to better understand some things about myself. Growing up, I was close to someone who was very introverted. I saw her isolation, and I felt such intense loneliness for her. I don't think she felt these same longings, but because of the way I was wired, I just couldn't accept this state of being for anyone.

Then there was my older sister, only fourteen months ahead of me, who was loved by everyone. She was incredibly fun, loving, and easy to get along with. I remember the first year that she left our small country town and went off to the big city for a youth camp. She came back with photo albums full of her hugging and laughing with every person on that camp. That was just the way she was.

When my turn came the following year, I expected to have the exact same experience. But I am just not her. I'm not great at small talk. I don't know what it is, but I find it a hard to get conversations going at times, and I can be very shy with people I don't know. I also have a higher dose of the awkward nerd factor than she does.

I remember many times when my friends came over to hang out with me and ended up spending a lot of time enjoying her company, then kicking on to a party with her afterward. We are just different. But some of these experiences planted deep insecurities in my heart about my acceptance and worth. My son's diagnosis helped me to see that because of this, I had placed a very high value on being accepted socially.

I applied this kind of "value economy" to the people around me. Those who had the kind of social skills I idolized were elevated to the highest status, and those that didn't were demoted. This affected the way I treated others in a subtle way, but more than that, it had a huge effect on my internal world. The people who ruled in my value economy were the ones who were worth my time.

As I came to understand this, I was deeply grieved. I had been standing in judgment over my son, and others, for their lack of ability in this area because of scars that ran deep from my younger years. I have spent time apologizing to God for this messed up way of thinking that resulted in much unkindness towards others. I had to ask him to change my heart and help me to have his value economy instead. Without it, I couldn't have learned to truly enjoy my son again.

The Truth About Our Worth

The Bible tells us that as God went about the business of making everything good in this universe, he climaxed his creative masterpiece with humans. And he declared, with pride and joy, that they were made "in his image." This has been the bearing I have used to reset my thinking. Humans are not valuable because of the things they do but because of who they are. You and I were made to know and reflect God in all his goodness. Our true worth comes from this truly incredible design and purpose.

So now, every day is an opportunity for me to enjoy my son just as he is. We're engaged in a therapy model that uses play to build meaningful connections. This helps him want to join us in a world of shared and enjoyed relationships more and more. We have had to relearn how to play. Somehow, years of adulting had stripped us of this ability. This holistic therapy approach regularly brings our whole family much joy.

The dark seasons of difference, diagnosis, and dead dreams can drain every last drop of hope from our hearts. And that was just what I needed. My hope for my son's future was in something so superficial and fleeting. It has now been replaced with a secure, lasting, and unimaginably greater hope.

My hope for my son is now in Jesus—that as he gets to know his Savior, he will choose to follow him. And if he does, it will open the door to a life that goes beyond this one, beyond disability, and beyond death, and on to a new life of wholeness through Jesus. And when I have that end game in mind, the dead dreams of today seem like nothing compared to what the future holds. Dreams for my son greater than I could ever imagine lie ahead because of what Jesus has done for us all. Life still throws us curveballs, but when I take the time to stop, lift my head, and look up to our glorious maker, I always find my hope is restored. And the hope he wants to fill our hearts with is so much greater than what we can so easily settle for.

> That is why we never give up. Though our bodies are dying, our spirits are being renewed every day. For our present troubles are small and won't last very long. Yet they produce for us a glory that vastly outweighs them and will last forever! So we don't look at the troubles we can see now; rather, we fix our gaze on things that cannot be seen. For the things we see now will soon be gone, but the things we cannot see will last forever. (2 Corinthians 4:16–18)

Renew and Restore

- Can you think of any "lesser" hopes that you are holding on to for yourself or your family?
- There is a greater hope, the hope that will be fulfilled by God alone, the one with which you can replace your lesser hope. How can you apply that to a disappointment that you're currently experiencing?
- What are some Bible passages that you can spend time feeding your soul with to help you to put your hope where it truly, securely belongs?

Jodie Cooper is an incredible sinner saved by a more incredible God. After years of painful misunderstandings about the Christian life, a crisis in her marriage finally led her to understand the gospel and its power to change lives. She now produces kid's books with resources to connect faith to daily life, and her YouTube channel, the *Gospel Led Family*, provides biblical encouragement for parents on their family discipleship journey. good-news-in-the-gum-trees-1.jimdosite.com

Accepting the Big Picture

Shannon Anderson

Sometimes life can feel like a jigsaw journey. God knows how all of the puzzle pieces fit together because he created it, but we don't get to see the "box lid" for the big picture. We have to trust that God will guide us to where we should place the pieces we are given. I'd chosen the word "trust" as my word for the year in 2020.

A New Year and New Path

It was my twenty-fifth year of teaching, and I felt as if I was at the peak of my career. I had been named one of the Top 10 Teachers who inspired the *Today Show* the week before. My writing and speaking work was really taking off too. My first two books for teachers had released, and I had three children's books coming out in the fall, followed by two more books in the spring.

I never thought in a hundred years that I would be published, let alone have five books coming out in the span of one year. I also had my entire summer booked with speaking invitations for conferences and events. I was even starting to get invitations for the start of the next school year. It seemed that 2020 was the year I should take a sabbatical leave from teaching to write, speak, and explore opportunities.

I prayed for discernment and felt at peace with my decision to request the 2020–2021 school year off. The school board approved my request, and I was filled with excitement and anticipation. I started contacting more organizations about speaking and principals about author visits. My situation was good. The puzzle pieces were starting to make sense.

In February, my husband and I got pretty sick. We both had terrible coughs that lingered for weeks. Lots of my students missed school. I ended up with a high fever and missed three days in a row, which had never happened before. We all figured it was the flu.

Unexpected Turn of Events

Spring forward, no pun intended, to March. News was spreading about this Coronavirus sickness. It was a mystery at the time, and we were oblivious to the fact that it may have been what we had experienced the month before. I remember my students and I were in the Maker-Space room working on some projects when the teachers all received a text that spring break was going to begin a week early and last for three weeks.

Schools around us had closed or gone virtual by this point in time. When I told my students that afternoon that they were leaving for a three-week spring break, there were tears. In all of our hearts, we knew that it was going to be longer than that. We knew we weren't coming back. With the exception of a couple of students, we all cried and hugged on the way to the bus lines that day.

The weeks of spring break were filled with unknowns. I received emails daily with postponements and cancellations of the various events I was supposed to be going to in the summer and fall. I actually called my principal and asked if I could rescind my sabbatical leave request. He gently told me that the position had already been filled and approved.

I felt as though someone took this puzzle I'd been working on for so long and flipped the table it was on. Pieces were strewn all around the room in a jumbled mess. How was I going to take a year off with no pay and no insurance? I would have no speaking income. To make matters worse, the reality hit that our speculations had been correct. We were *not* coming back to school. The rest of the year was virtual. I cannot explain how that felt. All of us teachers tried the best we could, but it was far from ideal. I was so worried about the kids and their emotional state, yet my mental state was probably just as fragile. It definitely isn't how I wanted the school year to end.

Hard Times

I clung to my faith. I prayed for a glimpse of the big picture, the "box lid." It wasn't long before even the churches were closing. Did God give me pieces to the wrong puzzle? Why was it getting so hard? When other people go through a hard time, I always tell them that God's plan is perfect and that we have to trust his timing and why things happen the way they do. I tried to follow my own advice. After all, my word for the year was "trust," right?

I was holding a few edge pieces and a few middle pieces of the puzzle. I needed to wait for other pieces to be given to me before I would be able to understand how they all fit together. Sometimes, it feels as if God takes a piece away from me, but I've noted he always provides another opportunity that fits when the time is right. While we are waiting for God to complete our picture, we can be supportive of others who are also waiting. We can look outside of ourselves and offer empathy, love, and encouragement.

Hope for Better Times

During my search, I discovered an online platform that needed more teachers. Most of the students were homeschooled, but many were public school kids who were behind because of the virtual learning experience.

I decided that may be a way I could help others and also earn a little income. It was also becoming clear that conference organizers were struggling to continue their work. I reached out to many and ended up with several keynote and featured speaking experiences. I was even invited to speak for a national conference.

Unexpected Blessings

Although I kept wishing that these presentations could be in person, I realized that if they had remained that way, I would not have been able to do the number of events I was doing. For example, there was one week that I was speaking for events in three different states. Logistically, that could have never happened if they were all in person because of the travel required.

I started to look for blessings through the pandemic, like the fact that my daughter, who is a senior in college and getting married after graduation, was home with us for many months. My online work was thriving. I was even able to hold an outdoor book launch event in the fall when two of my books released. I also had a homeschool group ask me to do writing lessons at the park for many weeks.

Something many of us have learned through this pandemic is that the pieces we are given are not always what we ask for or want. What we think the big picture should be may be completely off. I definitely felt like my word of the year was wrong, but it couldn't have been more right. I needed to learn to trust. My understanding of the puzzle is flawed, but my God is perfect. He knows what he's doing and how it will all come together in the end. That's what's important.

My word for 2021 is "purpose." I'm not going to keep wishing I were part of a different puzzle. I'm going to stick with what God has given me and discover my purpose as I continue to grow in faith and share it with others. Someday, I will get to see the big picture, and what a glorious sight that will be.

Renew and Restore

- In what ways have you had to trust that your puzzle pieces are the ones you are supposed to have?
- What do you feel your purpose for your part of the puzzle is?
- What pieces have fallen into place? How do you know?

Shannon Anderson is an award-winning teacher, author, and national speaker from Indiana. She was named one of the Top 10 Teachers who inspired the *Today Show*, and one of her recent books made it to #1 on the Amazon best-seller list. You can learn more about Shannon and her books at www.shannonisteaching.com

Loved Down to The Inch

Susan Macias

Sometimes, I don't pray for my own personal desires because they seem too trivial. After all, wars, famine, and injustice occur around the planet. Certainly, my inconveniences and petty difficulties don't matter in the grand scheme of things. But several instances in my life have taught me that the Lord cares about my small issues as well as the large ones. Experiencing those moments, more than anything else, has helped me see how much he loves me.

One such lesson occurred eighteen years ago, but I've never forgotten it. During twenty years of military life, we'd had seven children and moved eleven times. At each new location, we knew we wouldn't be settled for more than a few years. So, I'd quickly set things up and make them work as best as I could. We experienced a variety of homes during our military adventure, and we loved living in different places. But I dreamed of one day having a home that fit our family and its unique needs where we could unpack and stay.

A New Home

When my husband retired, our family moved home to Texas. We wanted to find a place and never move again. With unique needs, the house search dragged on. We traipsed all around the hill country of Texas, looking for just the right place. We required enough space for our big family and hoped for some acreage, with a price tag we could afford.

Along with enough bedrooms and bathrooms, we needed space that accommodated homeschooling. We'd already schooled at home for twelve years and had many more years of education ahead of us. Finally, after an intensive search, we found the perfect dwelling nestled in the middle of eight acres. Well, sort of perfect, as long as you ignored the dark wood paneling and 1970s light fixtures. All that was required were gallons of paint and hours of hard work, which made a vast improvement.

There was a perfect room we could dedicate entirely to homeschooling. No longer would we need to scuttle books off the dining room table so we could eat dinner. This lovely, light-filled space was long and thin with enough square feet for all the desks we required. It also contained a bank of windows that lined the back wall, affording a view of our backyard where the deer loved to graze. Between each window was the perfect amount of space for a bookshelf. I could just imagine how beautiful it would look and how functional it would be. But when I went to price six bookshelves, my heart sank. With our big family and a decrease in pay, we needed to tighten our belts everywhere we could. And after updating the house, no money remained for new furnishings.

I examined our current, garage-saled, mismatched assortment of bookshelves. Besides being the wrong size, their different looks and proportion didn't fit the vision. Could I ask the Lord for something so trivial? Honestly, my faith wasn't up to believing he'd provide that many identical shelves. A particular Scripture kept nudging my doubt. I could hear it echoing through my mind, "And if God cares so wonderfully for wildflowers that are here today and thrown into the fire tomorrow, he will certainly care for you. Why do you have so little faith?" (Matthew 6:30). Convicted, though not yet really believing God would answer, I tentatively asked, "Lord, we need bookshelves. And could they please match?"

A few weeks later, a new friend in the church we'd just begun attending mentioned that they were replacing some furniture, and they had an entire collection of white bookshelves. Since we had just moved into a new house, would we perhaps need them? They weren't fancy, but they were all white and in decent shape, and they had more than we even needed. I both jumped with joy and hung my head in shame. How had I not believed my heavenly Father cared as much about bookshelves as I did? He delights in giving his children gifts, and I hadn't trusted that. After a quick confession and apology, I thanked God profusely and hugged the woman he'd used to fulfill my heart's desire.

When Things Don't Fit

The next week, these generous friends delivered the coveted bookshelves to our home. I began placing them in between the windows. As each one slid in its intended spot, I beamed. It was just as I'd imagined. It almost had a library feel. That is, until we reached the last two windows. This time, the shelf wouldn't slide into the space. Confused, I measured again and discovered that between these two windows, the space was one inch less than the others. And therefore, one inch short of the shelf.

I felt devastated. I knew I should be grateful for what I had: four matching bookshelves. But there were five slots between the windows. Every time I walked into the room, I hated the blank white wall without a shelf. My vision of our schoolroom felt cheated.

For several days, I sulked. My husband thought he'd try to encourage me. "Honey, at least we have four. That's better than before."

I withheld the snarky response I wanted to blurt out. I didn't need to be reminded that what we had was sufficient. I knew it was. Not perfect, but enough. Instead of seeing what I'd received, I complained to the Lord. "Jesus, why almost give me what I asked for? It seems a bit unfair, if you want to know the truth." Slowly, those moaning-to-Jesus sessions became prayers. I needed his help to be grateful. And just maybe, he could provide a solution?

A few days later, the thought occurred to me: there were still some shelves in the garage. When they delivered more shelves than we needed, our friends told us to give away the extras. The shelves looked the same, so I'd assumed they were all identical. I couldn't imagine that one would be different, but I grabbed a tape measure and went to investigate. The first and second shelves measured identical to the bookshelves that already sat in the house—thirty-six inches wide.

But when I measured the third shelf, I just stared at the number on the tape. It wasn't thirty-six, but thirty-five inches wide. The exact dimension I needed.

I must have measured that shelf ten times to make sure my desire wasn't determining the number. But it really was a thirty-five-inch shelf. I called my boys to fetch the shelf from the garage, and they carried it inside, where it slid perfectly into the empty spot.

I stood back to observe my fulfilled vision of what I'd desired for that room to look like. Each window streamed light and was interspersed with a bookshelf, perfectly fitting the space between, as if handmade for the spot. I cried. And I apologized to Jesus, again, for not trusting him.

Down to The Inch

Why had I doubted the Lord, who knows when I come and go, the thoughts of my heart, and the exact number of hairs on my head? I'm not sure. But this tangible lesson drove home the fact that my Lord truly loves me down to the inch. Certainly, he's in the middle of my big issues. But he also cares about my small concerns, the ones that don't affect the fate of the world but bless my heart.

He cares for you the same way. Just as your problems aren't too big for Jesus to fix, they're also not too small for him to care about. He supplies my needs, and he will supply yours completely. Sometimes, in unique ways and with a few bumps along the way. But he does it perfectly. Down to the inch.

Renew and Restore

- Is it hard to ask Jesus for the small needs you experience? Why do you think that is?
- Think of needs in your life that seem trivial. Why not spend some time asking the Lord for help with those? What would change if you asked him for these types of things more often?

Susan Macias writes and speaks to train up an army of women in the second half of life to serve the kingdom, confidently follow Jesus, and fight offensively in prayer. Her award-winning book *UNCEASING: A Parent's Guide to Conquer Worry and Pray with Power* is available on Amazon, as is her prayer devotional, *31 Days Praying for My Daughter*. Find Susan at her blog, susankmacias.com, or on her podcast, *We're Not Done Yet!*

Afterword

On behalf of the authors in this book, I encourage you to take a next step. What is your repurposed story? I hope you are inspired by each of these stories to change your perspective in some way. Perhaps you've found courage and hope to pursue healing and restoration. More than writing words, we want to make a difference.

If you haven't taken a step of faith, or you're unsure about your relationship with Jesus, I invite you to make that your first step. Let me make it simple.

1. God wants a relationship with each of us. But we have a problem. Our sin separates us from that relationship, and we could never become good enough on our own to erase our sin or pay the debt it has caused.

2. Good news! There is a solution. Jesus offered to pay the penalty we owe, and he offers the gift of freedom from that debt.

3. You don't have to clean up any of the mess first. He wants you to approach him just as you are.

4. There is no formula. Just talk to God in your own words. Acknowledge your sin and regret. Tell him you'd like to receive the gift Jesus offers and start over. Commit to pursuing a life of following Jesus Christ and becoming more like him.

5. Celebrate! Tell someone. Write to one of us or tell a friend. Rejoice because this is a wonderful step. Ask someone to be your encourager as you continue to make that commitment solid and as life continues throwing challenges your way—because they will come.

Do you need more encouragement and inspiration? You'll notice that almost every writer has shared a blog, a podcast, or a social media connection. If you find them online and subscribe to their email lists, read articles, and listen to podcast episodes, you'll discover a treasure trove of content to help you continue to build your relationship with Jesus and navigate life's twists and turns.

Gratitude

Lastly, I owe so many thanks to all of the contributors in this book. Thank you for opening up your lives, for being vulnerable, and telling of your struggles and victories. I'm honored to have been able to introduce others to your authentic stories of repurposed life. May God continue to bless your writing as you point others to Jesus.

This is starting to feel like a graduation speech, but doesn't it need to end with a prayer or a blessing or something? Indeed. I know the perfect one.

> When I think of all this, I fall to my knees and pray to the Father, the Creator of everything in heaven and on earth. I pray that from his glorious, unlimited resources he will empower you with inner strength through his Spirit. Then Christ will make his home in your hearts as you trust in him. Your roots will grow down into God's love and keep you strong. And may you have the power to understand, as all God's people should, how wide, how

long, how high, and how deep his love is. May you experience the love of Christ, though it is too great to understand fully. Then you will be made complete with all the fullness of life and power that comes from God.

Now all glory to God, who is able, through his mighty power at work within us, to accomplish infinitely more than we might ask or think. Glory to him in the church and in Christ Jesus through all generations forever and ever! Amen.

Ephesians 3:14–21

Go boldly, life joyfully, and experience life, repurposed.

Michelle

For copies of this book and additional resources from the authors:

liferepurposedbook.com

Life Repurposed
Podcast and Community

with *Michelle Rayburn*

Life, Repurposed Podcast

Find uplifting and practical advice for everyday living, creative inspiration, and recommendations for books and resources that will encourage you to embrace your life, repurposed. Discover God in the midst of life's difficulties. New episodes come out weekly with a blend of guest interviews and solo shows.

Liferepurposed.me

Life, Repurposed Facebook Community

If you'd love to grow your connection with others on the repurposed adventure of life, you'll want to be part of the Life, Repurposed Facebook Community. Look for discussion and encouragement and meet friends to be inspired as we share our stories of transformation with each other.

facebook.com/groups/liferepurposed

About Destiny Rescue

A portion of the royalties from the sales of this book are donated to Destiny Rescue, an organization that is committed to rescuing kids from sexual exploitation and helping them stay free.

Since 2001, this organization has rescued more than 5900 individuals enslaved around the world, helped keep hundreds more from entering the sex trade through various human trafficking prevention programs, ensured justice for those who have been wronged, and raised awareness.

Readers are welcome to make additional donations or help to spread the word about the fundraiser.

See our progress here:

go.destinyrescue.org/liferepurposed

For more information about **Destiny Rescue**, go to

www.destinyrescue.org/us

Other Books
You Might Enjoy

by the Authors

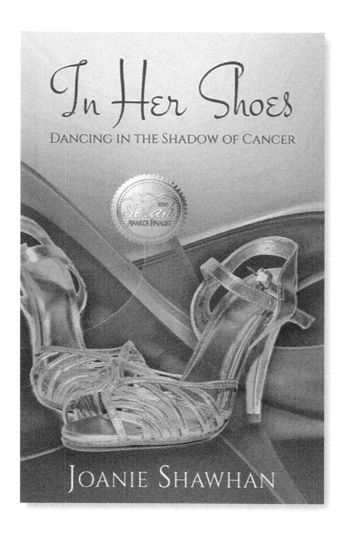

In Her Shoes: Dancing in the Shadow of Cancer

Frightened by cancer? Riddled with questions? Perhaps you or a loved one is battling this disease. Do you know where to turn for encouragement, comfort and support? *In Her Shoes—Dancing in the Shadow of Cancer* is a collection of vignettes, highlighting the stories of everyday women with everyday lives interrupted by cancer—their challenges, heartbreaks, questions, and triumphs. In these pages, you will find helpful tips, inspiration, and hope. Cancer is hard, but you are not alone.

www.joanieshawhan.com

LEAD YOUR FAMILY TO STAND IN AWE OF GOD

Glory

JODIE COOPER ~ MARIA RODRIGUEZ

Glory: Lead Your Family to Stand in Awe of God

A Family Discipleship Resource

The all-powerful, all-loving God of the universe can easily become much less than he is in our minds. *Glory* is a resource designed to help families of faith start important, life changing conversations about God's truth at home. Read the fun, beautifully illustrated story together then use the Family Discussion Guide and Action Project to help your kids discover how living for God's glory can change their lives today. You can find more resources like this from Jodie Cooper at her website.

good-news-in-the-gum-trees-1.jimdosite.com

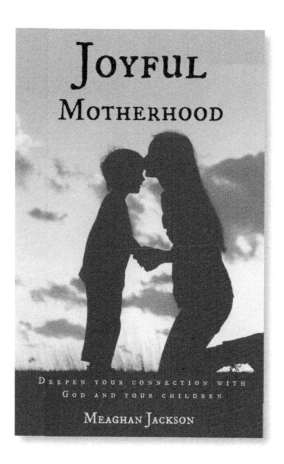

Joyful Motherhood

Deepen your connection with God and your children

Motherhood is one of the biggest blessings and challenges in a woman's life. The path to becoming a gentle, peaceful parent as a Christian is often wrought with overwhelm, anxiety, and guilt. God's Word is filled with encouragement and hope. Meaghan Jackson of Joyful Mud Puddles has prayerfully curated 31 days in God's word for mothers. This book is filled with scripture, wisdom, and questions to help you deepen your relationship with God and your children. As a working and homeschooling mom of three boys, Meaghan understands the busy mom life.

More books and Bible studies by Meaghan Jackson are coming soon.

www.joyfulmudpuddles.com/joyful-motherhood

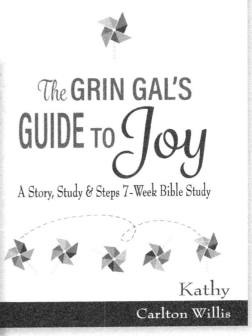

Did you know the trials Job endured are the same ones hitting us today? In *7 Trials Every Woman Faces*, author Kathy Carlton Willis explores the biblical view of trials and gives resources for you to handle trials as well as help others cope.

If you've ever felt like your joy has gone missing, *The Grin Gal's Guide to Joy* is for you! Each chapter shares stories and observations (Grin with Joy), Bible word study (Grow with Joy), life application steps (Go with Joy), and ways to share joy with others (Give with Joy).

Ideal for groups. Leader guide included.

www.kathycarltonwillis.com

Secrets of the Pastor's Wife: A Novel

Cassandra Martin lives in the quaint village of Maple Grove. The forty-something artist seems like the perfect wife for John Martin, the pastor at Maple Avenue Community Church.

But widow and coffee shop owner, Katherine Montague, senses that beautiful Cassie is haunted by a heartbreaking secret. She's praying to find a way to help her.

Will Cassie trust Katie with the pain of her past or will she let her secrets destroy her?

Entertaining and inspiring fiction from award-winning writer, Christina Ryan Claypool, recommended for Christian Women's Book Clubs featuring discussion questions.

www.christinaryanclaypool.com

#beyou

Change Your *Identity*
One Letter at a Time

Kolleen Lucariello

We often find ourselves held captive by an identity crisis when we allow relationships, titles, perceived success or the opinion of others to define us. What if you could finally experience a transformational victory over your identity struggles? Are you ready to believe and apply truth that activates the courage to conquer insecurities, inferiority, shame and self-doubt?

In the pages of this book you will discover how to walk away from false definitions and live with clear purpose and priorities. It is possible to change your identity and you can do it one letter at a time.

Available through Activ8Her.org

The Repurposed and Upcycled Life
Book and Participant Workbook

Are there experiences you'd rather toss in the dumpster? Discover the repurposed and upcycled life. With laugh-out-loud humor, Michelle will help you see how some of your greatest disappointments, mistakes, and hurts can be beautiful treasures from God. Move forward with new purpose, even in the midst of the trashy stuff of life.

Books by Michelle Rayburn include:

- *The Repurposed and Upcycled Life: When God Turns Trash to Treasure*
- *The Repurposed and Upcycled Life: A Women's Small Group Bible Study* (Workbook)
- *Classic Marriage: Staying in Love as Your Odometer Climbs*

www.michellerayburn.com

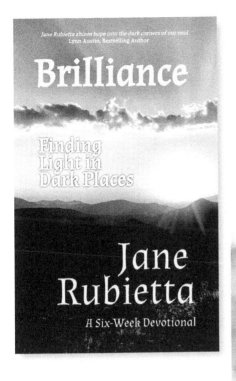

Brilliance: Finding Light in Dark Places

Need some light? Jane Rubietta's newest book leads us from the shadows into hope. Six weeks of emotive, applicable readings make this a book to read again, and great for gifts and groups. Because it's not good to be alone.

The Forgotten Life of Evelyn Lewis

Jane's award-nominated debut novel. When her carefully built life crumbles, Evelyn must unearth her past to build her future. Lots of humor, sweet tea, and hot summer sun.

A prolific author, Jane Rubietta speaks internationally. She loves helping people live their best lives.

See **JaneRubietta.com** for more.

Made in the USA
Monee, IL
21 March 2021